Lincolnshire Fens

– Landscapes and Legends –

Text by Alan Stennett

Paintings by Mo Teeuw

Cottage
Publications

First published by Cottage Publications,
an imprint of Laurel Cottage Ltd.
Donaghadee, N. Ireland 2010.
Copyrights Reserved.
© Illustrations by Mo Teeuw 2010.
© Text by Alan Stennett 2010.
All rights reserved.
No part of this book may be reproduced or stored on any media
without the express written permission of the publishers.
Design & origination in Northern Ireland.
Printed & bound in China.
ISBN 978 1 900935 87 6

The Author

Alan Stennett is a writer and broadcaster who spent his early years in the village of Billingborough on the edge of the Lincolnshire Fens, an area in which his family have farmed for at least five generations.

Alan was part of the team who set up BBC Radio Lincolnshire in 1980, and produced and presented a wide range of programmes about the county before leaving to go freelance in 1994. He now specialises in writing and broadcasting about Lincolnshire and its agriculture. His previous books covered the local dialect, the county's lost railways and the changes in agriculture seen there over the past 100 years.

He now lives with his wife, Sue, in an old railway station on the banks of the River Witham close to the site of the great Fenland monastery at Kirkstead.

The Artist

Mo Teeuw is a professional artist and tutor. Born in London and educated in Somerset, Mo taught art at Secondary School level before working in Adult Education.

Mostly self-taught, Mo has worked alongside some of the UK's foremost artists. As well as running workshops and demonstrating to local art groups Mo also runs residential courses at Dedham Hall, Suffolk, Holt Hall, Norfolk, Marlborough College, Wiltshire and takes painting holidays in France, Spain and Morocco.

She has been made an associate member of the British Watercolour Society and is an exhibiting member of the Welland Valley Art Society, Norfolk Art Circle, East Coast Artists and The Lincolnshire Artists Society. Mo also exhibits at the Mall Gallery and with the Society of Women Artists

Mo takes a lighthearted approach to teaching, as she firmly believes that learning should be fun, but that does not mean she isn't serious about her art. Further information on her work and courses can be found at www.moteeuw.co.uk.

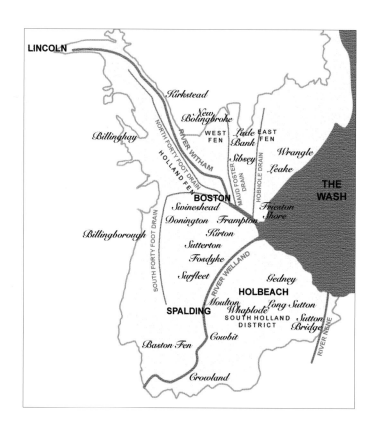

LINCOLN

Kirkstead

New Bolingbroke

Billinghay

WEST FEN

Little Bank

EAST FEN

Sibsey

Wrangle

Leake

NORTH FORTY FOOT DRAIN

RIVER WITHAM

HOLLAND FEN

MAUD FOSTER DRAIN

HOBHOLE DRAIN

THE WASH

BOSTON

Swineshead

Frieston Shore

Donington

Frampton

Billingborough

Kirton

Sutterton

Fosdyke

SOUTH FORTY FOOT DRAIN

RIVER WELLAND

Surfleet

Gedney

HOLBEACH

SPALDING

Moulton

Long Sutton

Whaplode

SOUTH HOLLAND DISTRICT

Sutton Bridge

RIVER NENE

Baston Fen

Cowbit

Crowland

THE SOUTH LINCOLNSHIRE FENS SHOWING MAIN DRAINAGE PATTERNS

Contents

Welcome to the Fens

~~

The Lincolnshire Fens are what gives the whole county its reputation. Ask anyone to describe Lincolnshire, and you will be told it is flat, much to the frustration of those Yellerbellies – natives of the county – who live in the rolling landscape of the Wolds, the Lincolnshire Heath or the Lincoln Edge. On the Fens, however, the description is entirely accurate. Great sweeps of prime agricultural land stretch from flat horizon to flat horizon, with the whole dominated by the great dome of sky that is the pride of those of us who love this open country.

The contribution of the Fens to the image of Lincolnshire is even more surprising when you consider that its third of a million acres is only about a fifth of that of the whole historic county. Like all true locals, I will disregard the attempts to slice away part of the north, first to Humberside, then to the unitary councils of North and North-East Lincolnshire. To me, the county runs 'fra the Wesh to th'Umber and the Trent to the Noth Seeya' as the local dialect would have it.

Historically, much of the Fens were not only flat, they were also wet. If you go back a few hundred years, the coast itself was much further inland to the west of the Wash, where the Welland and the Glen emptied into a bigger estuary near Bicker. There they were joined by the Witham, which flowed into what is still called Bicker Haven until it broke through to its current course through Boston, possibly during the great floods of 1014. I have seen some wonderful LIDAR images – a kind of air-borne combination of lasers and radar that can penetrate into the soil – that shows the old courses of the Witham as a great skein of channels weaving their way down from Lincoln to what would have been the coast. The road across the fen from Martin to my home near Kirkstead Bridge is known as 'the bumpy road' by my grandchildren as it bucks and rears over different soil types into which the road has sunk to varying levels.

A lot of the ground of the Fens hardly qualified as dry land – it consisted largely of marsh and bog, as water that drained into it from the higher ground to the north and west flowed away very slowly, if at all. The current landscape is almost entirely the result of centuries of patient work done by generations of locals trying to protect their homes and farms from all that water, and later by enthusiastic landowners with a dream of great fields of crops, supported by engineers and workmen, usually equipped with nothing more sophisticated that a shovel and a wheelbarrow.

Several other parts of Lincolnshire have also been reclaimed from the waters, including the Isle of Axholme in the north-west, the Ancholme Valley running north to the Humber and the Lincolnshire Marsh, stretching down the North Sea coast from the famous fishing port of Grimsby to south of our premier sea-side resort, Skegness, but the South Lincolnshire Fens are the largest such area.

In broad terms they run north from the Norfolk and Cambridgeshire county boundaries, with their western edge just 'downhill' of the line of towns and villages that sit on the edge of the Heath from Stamford and Bourne through to Digby. They follow the line of what is believed to be an old Roman channel called the Carr Dyke, which curves back south around the Billinghay 'promontory' before continuing north to Lincoln. From Lincoln, the boundary returns south along the other side of the Witham valley, passing Bardney, Woodhall and Tattershall before swinging east along the southern edge of the Lincolnshire Wolds. The division between the Fens and the Marsh is a bit arbitrary, but is usually taken to be the present course of the Steeping River, which rises on the Wolds and empties into the sea near Wainfleet.

Most of the land is at or below mean sea level, which means that it would flood almost instantaneously if the sea defences were removed, or the rivers, which usually flow at above the level of the land, had their raised banks breached. I have watched the Witham flow past my house at a level which would correspond with a point half-way up the downstairs windows, and we live in an old railway station which was deliberately built on raised banks to keep it above the worst flood risks. A friend driving further south, on the Holbeach Marsh, where the land is several feet below tide level, claimed that his sophisticated diving equipment, left turned on the in the back of his car, suddenly piped up to tell him that he should check his air tanks, since it reckoned he had been underwater too long!

The end result of all that digging and draining is one of the world's great farmed landscapes. Whatever time of year you choose to go out, something will be being harvested somewhere. Harvest to most people means grain, and we grow a lot of grain in the Fens, but for us the term can include virtually everything that can be grown on what is some of the finest soils in the world. The flowers that bloom in the spring (tra-la) in the rest of the country are harvested for nearly half the year in Lincolnshire. A substantial proportion of the country's potatoes are grown here, as is beet for sugar production and oilseed rape and linseed for their oils. We grow most of the cabbages and cauliflowers eaten in Britain, as well as that finest of all winter vegetables, the brussel sprout, or, as a leading local grower insists, the British sprout! There are some strange people who dislike this splendid vegetable, to which I can only reply – all the more for me, then.

The variety of cropping is reflected in the ever changing landscape. Winter can be bleak, as an east wind drives snow directly into the faces of flower and vegetable pickers working with frozen fingers and cold feet to keep the flow of produce coming into the shops. The dull blue-green of cabbages can be the only colour in an otherwise grey and black landscape.

Spring, by contrast, can offer a blaze of colour. Ireland's forty shades of green is a miserable palette compared to a south Lincolnshire landscape in spring. The flower crops have their own gaudy splendour, but other fields glow with the yellow of rape, the glorious blue of linseed in flower and the pinks and mauves of some of the newer crops now being grown for specialist oils or pharmaceuticals.

A subtler shade of red can be detected in early summer as the barley crops ripen and the spiky awns on the developing ears catch the light and the wind to ripple like the waters that once would have covered the land. Yellow dominates later in the season as the main cereal crops ripen before the combine harvesters mow them down – ideally in glorious sun, but often caught in the dry spells between showers.

Autumn and winter harvesting digs deep into the soils to lift potatoes and sugar beet, and the fenland motorist needs to be aware that tractors, trailers and harvesters can leave mud slicks on the road to catch the unwary or inexperienced driver. It is not the prettiest time to visit the Lincolnshire Fens, although the tress that were often planted to shelter houses or farms can still offer a fine variety of colours to the passing traveller.

Although it is largely an arable farming landscape today, there are intriguing hints of an older style in the names of places and roads. Gedney Drove End is, logically, at the end of the drove from Gedney, and Whaplode Drove fills the same role for Whaplode, but what is a drove? When the Fens were wetter, their main use was for pasturing animals, which were moved onto the fen and marsh edges during the summer when the land dried and fresh grazing could be found. To get there, they were driven along droves – wide roadways along which a herd or flock could move while under the control of a farmworker, possibly with the aid of a dog. Many of them are still known by the names of what were previously landowners or farmers, but just who Tye, Swain, Stong or Hallam were we will never know, unless a descendant is still living in the area. Others go by jobs, like Washdyke Drove, or locations, such as Vicarage Drove, but Labour in Vain Drove on the Billinghay Fen can only have been named by someone severely disillusioned with life on the fens, or perhaps he had just had a bad day with his sheep.

Driving on the Fens can be a frustrating experience, particularly for someone like me; an agricultural journalist who has to find individual farms or smaller communities. Some roads are wonderfully direct – the 7-mile straight and the 5-mile straight through New Bolingbroke and New York are perfectly accurately named, but others wind and twist along older routes that had to avoid the wettest holes. When Dr Beeching proposed the closure of the railway line serving Skegness, among the arguments that saved the service was that the main road from Boston, the A52, was so tortuous that it couldn't carry the increased traffic. In addition, the whole area is criss-crossed by hundreds of drainage channels, and bridges aren't always where you want them. There are only four crossings over the Witham between Lincoln and Boston and just one over the Nene in Lincolnshire. The Glen, the Slea, the Welland and the major drains can also cause you to make long diversions, often between places that are perfectly visible from one another. Near Whaplode Drove, I had to drive for three miles to find a bridge to get me to the farm that I could see less than a hundred yards away on the other side of a drain.

Historically, most of the older settlements were on the drier stretches of land close to the coast, or where the coast was when they were established, and they are still the densest areas of population. To the north and west most of the population lived just off the Fens themselves, and went down onto them to farm or to fowl or to fish, although Market Deeping and Donington were both out from the fen edge, and served as market towns to the western Fens. Some communities did develop within the Fens themselves, but life there could be risky and unpleasant. Two hundred years ago, one writer described Chapel Hill as being *'inaccessible, but by boat or by riding horse belly-deep, more in water than mud'* and the neighbouring parish of Dogdyke where *'not two houses* [were] *communicable for whole winters round, and sometimes scarcely in summer'.*

The situation has changed since draining, but most of the settlements have been small. Some, like New Bolingbroke, were deliberately 'planted' in the hope of becoming an important centre. The village took the market rights from Old Bolingbroke on the Wolds edge, and boasts a surprising crescent of fine houses in its centre, but it failed to prosper, although it still supports an engineering firm that specialises in the exotic field of the manufacture and repair of fairground rides as well as more conventional machinery. Others grew up around what had previously been single farms or tiny communities on land that had been a little drier in their undrained state. The 'hills' on which Chapel Hill, Hill Dyke, Clark's Hill, Penny Hill and Weston Hills may not be discernible to the naked eye, but they would certainly have felt different to the badly shod foot.

By far the biggest group, though, are the offshoots of existing villages on land which originally belonged to them. Holbeach spun off Holbeach St. Marks and Holbeach St. Matthew onto the reclaimed marsh and Holbeach St. Johns onto the inland fens. Each new centre has a church dedicated to their respective saint, and built during the nineteenth century as the population expanded. Long Sutton, Gedney and Moulton founded similar clusters, while Leake, to the north of Boston, has a counterpart, New Leake, right in the middle of the East Fen.

The two largest towns, Boston and Spalding, are to be found at the lowest available crossing points on the Witham and the Welland respectively, and grew up as ports as well as regional communication centres and market towns. At about 30,000 inhabitants each, they are both still key local centres, supplying most of the needs of the surrounding villages.

I have a great affection for Boston, dating back to the times when, as a very small boy, I was taken to visit two of my father's elderly aunts, who lived in the town. The fond memories, though, were not of the ladies, who were a rather forbidding pair, but of being allowed to walk into the town to Central Park to see the budgerigars in a line of large cages near to the entrance. The cages and the budgerigars – or their descendants – are still there, and I took the opportunity to remake their acquaintance during a series of radio outside broadcasts that took place from the park. My colleagues were a little surprised at my enthusiasm for the display…

Nowadays we visit regularly for the market, still held in the very fine historic marketplace, overlooked by the great tower of St. Botolph's church, universally known as the Stump. The neighbouring farming ensures an excellent supply of fresh produce to the market, supplemented by material from the packhouses in the area, which deal with imported produce as well as local material.

The town also offers what the local council refer to as a Cultural Quarter, based around the Blackfriars Theatre, Sam Newsom Music Centre and the town museum located in the 14th century Guild Hall, which may have been the location of the trial and imprisonment of the Pilgrim Fathers during their first, unsuccessful, attempt to leave Britain for the New World.

Spalding is the major centre for packing and processing food and flowers. Shortly before a family wedding, my wife, Sue, went down to the flower market in the town and bought all the requirements for the marquee and the table decorations at a fraction of the cost of having them made for the event. The town holds another early 'shopping' memory for me, which might be seen as a contributory factor to my present career. At about the age of ten I was taken to a pre-Christmas toy display in a shop in the town, and allowed to choose a gift. I picked out a John Bull printing outfit, which allowed me to set rubber type in a wooden holder and stamp out my own printed documents. The maximum printed area was about an inch by two inches, and there was a regrettable shortage of some key letters, but it did give me a very early taste of journalism.

There are those who find the Lincolnshire Fens bleak and inhospitable, a view with which many of those workers in the winter fields might well agree. The Lincolnshire dialect is packed with words for rain. If it isn't actually raining, it could be doley or mawky, gradually developing through mizzlin to drinjy and owery right through to teemin, putherin, juggin, silin or skelchin if you really get caught in a heavy storm – and that's only about half of the possible terms. There are fewer ways of describing a really sunny day – a razzler would be one – but we would argue that that has nothing to do with a shortage of such days, just that we are too busy enjoying it to do much talking about it!

The landscape by day can also seem very empty, with miles of fields, and very few signs of habitation, but that changes dramatically at night, when hundreds of house lights show where the dwellings were previously hidden by shelter belts of trees or just tucked away as individual buildings or in small clusters.

That same night can also demonstrate another of the advantages of our big skies. The nights here are dark, so the stars can be splendid, as can a glorious dawn over the coast and a fantastic bullfinch sky – a blaze of red at sunset.

The Lincolnshire Fens are a landscape you need to learn to live with, but if you take that trouble it will pay you back a thousand fold. The small pleasures of glimpses of a kingfisher taking its prey from behind a sluice a few hundred yards from home, watching barn owls sweep along the drain banks in one of their most welcoming territories, enjoying the daffodils planted on so many roadsides or the fields of tulips on my way to work, or the bigger ones of the changing colours of the fields or the movement of cloud shadows across the waterways are all part of the attractions of the Fens. Best of all, though, is the feeling of belonging. My family have farmed the Fens for at least five generations, and although I never took to tilling the land, it is, and always will be, home.

The North Forty-Foot Drain, which runs from near Billinghay to join the Witham at Boston, collects much of the water flowing off Holland Fen, but it wasn't the first waterway to be dug along that route. In 1720, Earl Fitzwilliam, who owned a lot of badly drained land near Billinghay, set out to try to improve it by cutting his own channel through the Fen.

Sadly, the project was something of a disaster. His tenants didn't find it made things better, so they cut the banks to let the water flow out onto Holland Fen, presumably to the great irritation of anyone already farming there. The new cut also provided a convenient alternative outlet for the Witham river waters, which flowed into the Drain near Chapel Hill and continued down it to Boston. The loss of water to the main channel was so great that an engineer visiting the area in 1761 reported that the river bed was so dry that it was being farmed, while the land on either side was regularly flooded until it became *'noxious and unwholesome to the adjacent inhabitants'*.

The changes also meant that shipping could no longer use the river, so a major scheme was designed and implemented that straightened the waterway, raised its banks, erected a new Grand Sluice at Boston and installed locks to improve the navigation. The Forty-Foot was also cleared and straightened, leaving the main pattern of drainage as we see it now.

It still wasn't perfect – in 1799 the floods were so bad that many crops were harvested by men in boats, with some only accessible by *'men standing up to their waists in water, clipping off the ears wherever they peeped above the surface'*. That hasn't happened for some time, but we all still keep an eye on the water levels whenever there is heavy rain in the county.

The North Forty-Foot Drain

LORD FITZWILLIAM'S DRAIN

The Fenland waterways have always been used by boats. A hollowed-out log from prehistoric times has been found on the banks of the Witham, and for most of the time that people have lived in the Fens the only way to get to some locations would have been by water. The Roman waterfront at Lincoln shows that, two thousand years ago, the city was at the centre of a network of waterways linking the sea, the Fens and the River Trent.

Waterways link many of the great Fenland monasteries, and medieval records show regular disputes between owners of watermills, fishermen, river boats and land drainers. The Court of Sewers, which governed such matters, must have been a very interesting place!

Market boats took produce to the waterside communities from the market towns, and individual farmers and growers took in their own butter and eggs to sell. A neighbour claims his father, trying to get an early place at Boston market, set out in his boat before sunrise. As dawn broke, he realised that he was still attached by a rope to his mooring post, and several hours of rowing had moved him all of six feet.

Horse-drawn packet boats ran for many years, but were displaced by steam boats, despite a rear-guard action of trying to block the river with their tow-lines to stop the faster steam vessels overtaking. In response, the steamers fitted knives to their bows, enabling them to cut through such blockades.

The traffic today is mainly pleasure craft; so numerous at summer weekends that they sometimes have to double park on the moorings. A scheme is under way to link Boston, through the Fenland drains, with the Nene near Peterborough, which will offer visitors a better view of our unique landscape.

Participants in the annual rowing race from Lincoln to Boston would probably like a more leisurely look at the countryside, but their backward facing view is usually of nothing more than high banks and fellow rowers. They still call it fun …

The Witham at Kirkstead

WATER TRAFFIC ON THE FENS

The village of New Bolingbroke lies on the Seven Mile Straight, one of two long straight roads running north-south across the reclaimed West Fen. Most of the buildings are what you would expect of a fairly typical fen settlement, except for the rather striking crescent of houses about half way along the main street. It is one of the relics of the three great dreams of John Parkinson. The land agent for Sir Joseph Banks, of Revesby, Parkinson set out to found a city, to dig a coal mine and to plant a forest – remarkable aims for the early 19th century! New Bolingbroke was to have been his city. He took the market rights held by the Wolds village of Old Bolingbroke, and transferred them to the new settlement, but there weren't enough people or industries in the area for it to grow beyond its present modest status.

The second scheme was more successful, but for the wrong reasons. Parkinson set miners to work in 1823 close to the fen edge near Kirkstead, but although they dug down 1200 ft no coal was found. Parkinson was declared bankrupt in 1826, but water from a spring 500 ft down filled the shaft and overflowed into a stream. According to the local story, cattle that drank from the stream were cured of an illness, and when the water was tested it proved to be high in mineral salts. A bath-house was built around the shaft, which became the source of the waters at Woodhall Spa. A Victorian spa town was laid out around the baths and, although never a city, it came much closer to Parkinson's dream that New Bolingbroke ever did.

Parkinson's forest did get started, but never actually achieved that status. Ostler's Plantation on Kirkby Moor still stands tribute to him, but only the most generous would call it a forest. It is named after a Mr Ostler, who bought the pine and oak plantation after Parkinson was declared bankrupt. That original woodland is long gone, but the plantation is now owned by the Forestry Commission and pines are the only trees to be found there.

New Bolingbroke

THE DREAMER OF NEW BOLINGBROKE

Lincolnshire is a windy county, a fact recognised by the London and North Eastern Railway when they described our seaside resorts as 'bracing'. That may have fooled the visitors to Skegness, but most locals would have less kindly words to describe an east wind coming across the Fens with nothing, according to an elderly relative of mine, between us and Siberia. A friend with an east-facing cottage near Midville called his house 'Hill View' on the grounds that he ought to have been able to see the Urals.

Throughout history, though, that wind has been put to practical use driving mills, and Lincolnshire has a particularly good selection still in operation, or recently restored by enthusiasts.

The Fens have their share of working mills, but, sadly, none of them were built for the main purpose to which wind power was put here; driving great scoop wheels which lifted water out of the land-level local drains into higher waterways that took it to a river or the sea. Since they were erected at crucial points on the drainage system, often fed by so-called 'engine drains', they were demolished and replaced by steam when that became the main motive power. Most of those have now also gone, to be replaced by diesel or electric pumps.

The windmills that remain, like the six-storey Sibsey Trader, now in the care of English Heritage, were all grain mills, producing flour and animal feed for their local communities. Many of them, including Sibsey and the fine Maud Foster Mill in Boston, still sell flour and even bake excellent bread, although it is worth remembering that the toothless nature of many old villagers had a lot more to do with stone grains in the flour than with too many sweets as children!

Sibsey Trader

WORKING THE WIND

Lade Bank Pumping Station is an outcrop of Victorian industry in the middle of the modern agricultural landscape of the Fens. A single-storey building made of red and yellow brick with slate roofs, it stands about half-way down the Hobhole Drain, a man-made canal that carries water from the East Fen to an outlet in Boston Haven, a couple of miles downstream from the town.

The East Fen was one of the biggest challenges to the engineer John Rennie, when he was commissioned to draw up plans for draining the Fens. An area in the north-east corner of the Fen was known as The Deeps, and, like the Norfolk Broads, it appears to have been where peat had been dug for fuel in pre-historic times. One part of it, the Cranberry Fen, would have met with the approval of modern health enthusiasts, since it produced vast quantities of the berries.

A lock had been built at Lade Bank in 1805, but the constant shrinking of the peat soils lowered the land surface. This meant that gravity alone would not carry the water to the sea, so pumps were installed in 1867 to raise it into the southern part of the drain. Those first pumps in the station were driven by steam engines fed by six coal-fired boilers. The tall square chimney built in an Italianate style to serve the boilers is still intact, and when I last visited, seemed to have been put to good use carrying the smoke from a bonfire of waste from the site.

The station was extended in 1938 with new facilities alongside the earlier building and oil engines were installed in 1940. Electric pumps were brought into use in 1963 and 1990.

Lade Bank

Pumping Station

DRAINING THE EAST FEN

A springtime culinary treat for Lincolnshire is the arrival of the first Boston new potatoes. The silt lands running north along the coast from Boston offer the ideal growing conditions for potatoes of all kinds, but the first harvests of the early varieties are something special. Slightly waxy in texture, and needing nothing more than a quick rub to dislodge any of the loose, paper-thin skin, they go straight into the pot with some fresh mint. Served with a knob of butter they are a meal in themselves, although the addition of a few stems of local asparagus, which fortunately appears at about the same time, also doused in melted butter, would be even better. Add some sage-rich Lincolnshire sausages, and you have a meal fit for a king!

Canny buyers know to disregard the shops that offer what I regard as the inferior 'new potatoes' from Jersey, Cornwall or such exotic locations as Egypt and Cyprus. They watch the roadsides instead, because the first indications of the Boston crop are always the small-scale growers who have coaxed their individual plots to yield just those few days earlier than the rest, then hand-dug them to ensure there is no harvesting damage. They can be guaranteed to make a good return on their investment of effort, since those one-pound paper bags will sell for two pounds or more – about half the price of a complete sack of 'old' main crop at the same time.

Those early prices only last a few days, but the lower prices that follow them are in no way an indication of lower quality.

For two or three weeks in spring the flavour and the quality lasts, so everyone gets the chance to enjoy them.

Following on to the new crop comes all the other stages of the potato harvest, one of Lincolnshire's most important crops, and one which played a key part in the development of commercial agriculture in the Lincolnshire Fens.

Potato lifting at Wrangle

BOSTON NEW POTATOES

The Wash, with its sand and mudbanks, tidal creeks and salt marshes, is a wonderful place for bird-watching and wildfowling. Nearly half a million birds can be found here at any one time, with up to four times that number passing through on their annual migrations. 'Twitchers' gather from all over the country to see great flocks of migratory species passing through during the spring and autumn. They can also observe many types that nest here throughout the year or over-winter on the marshes or the surrounding farmlands. Less than a mile from my home one February I counted over sixty swans sitting in a wheat field grazing on the crop. Flocks of Brent Geese doing the same can cause serious damage if the ground is wet and the birds pull up the plants rather than just eating the young shoots.

Great flocks of lapwings sometimes confuse people who know the bird is the symbol of the Lincolnshire Wildlife Trust due to its falling numbers in the county. However, those big flocks are just passing through, while the Trust wants more nesting and raising young here.

Farmlands on the Fens are also among the best places to see the ghostly shape of a barn owl drifting over a drain in search of small mammals for supper. Kingfishers flash over the waterways and a stately heron can often be seen patiently waiting for a fish to swim by.

The RSPB looks after two dedicated reserves on the Lincolnshire Wash shore, at Frampton Marsh and Frieston Shore, either side of the mouth of the Witham. These provide easy, but controlled, access to the birds, as well as offering fine locations for school visits and other educational activities.

A long-established tradition of the Fens is wildfowling, hunting for duck and other edible species. That tradition is still maintained around the Wash, and wildfowlers will tell you that nothing compares with watching the sun rise over the sea on a cold but clear winter morning.

Frieston Shore

FEED THE BIRDS

Boston's Market Place is still very much the heart of the town. Twice a week it fills with what is almost certainly the best street market in Lincolnshire. We head down there regularly to stock up with fruit and vegetables, both those locally grown and those from much further afield. I expect to find cauliflowers, cabbages, potatoes, salads, flowers, bulbs and the whole of the rest of the range of produce that Lincolnshire's fertile fields produce, but there are surprises to be found there as well. On our return from a holiday in China I jokingly asked the owner of one of the produce stalls if he had any lotus root – a regular component of our diet while we were away. "Oh yes," he replied, fishing it out of a bucket under the stall. "How much would you like?" My bluff was called – we had a stir fry with lotus root that night!

Apart from the produce, and the usual market traders offering socks, underwear, woollens, leather goods and backpacks, electronic gadgets, items offered on television shopping channels at a third of the price and semi-legal services involving mobile phones, there are less common offerings. One stall offers olives in a variety of dressings – not locally grown, he assured me, while another can provide all that is needed to keep your bike on the road and a third is well stocked with back issues of magazines you never previously knew existed. A fine market, with ample opportunities to buy, or to waste time.

On the days when there is no market, there is time to enjoy some attractive architecture. The Assembly Rooms were built in 1822 for dancing, entertainment and public events, and still fulfil the same function. I have spoken there on a number of occasions, and am always aware of the historic setting, and the fierce debates that must have been held there on occasion in the past.

Like so many country towns, Boston has seen its share of architectural vandalism in the past half century or so, with the demolition of the old Peacock and Royal Hotel a particular loss to the Market Place. The street level is mostly faced with uninspiring shop fronts, but a glance up to first floor level will show the variety of styles and periods still present in this old town.

Market Place, Boston

CAULIFLOWERS AND LOTUS ROOT

The church of St. Botolph in Boston is a truly magnificent structure. Its tower, standing 272 feet above the Fens, is the tallest non-cathedral church tower in the world, the church itself is the widest in England, the tallest to the roof and, although the popular local belief that it has the largest floor area in England is not true, it is certainly among the top half dozen. Visitors over the centuries have described it as 'the Lighthouse of the Fens', 'a magnificent testimony in stone' and 'a stunning vision', but to the locals it is simply, and very prosaically, known as 'the Stump'! Why the Stump? No-one really knows, although architectural historian Nikolaus Pevsner believes it is because the structure is unfinished, and a steeple should have been added to its already vertiginous height.

Many people think that the octagonal stone lantern on top of the tower was once literally that – a guiding light to mariners heading into the port and travellers crossing the often trackless wastes of the Fens – and although there is no actual evidence for that, it is certainly visible for many miles.

The present church, started in 1309, is not the first on the site, since the remains of an earlier Norman structure have been found. Early legends suggest that St. Botolph himself founded a monastery on the site in 654, but this is very doubtful.

The nave was completed in around 1390, but construction of the tower did not start for another 60 years, and took 70 more to finish. The foundations are reputed to be 35 feet deep, which means that most of their depth is well below that of the adjacent tidal River Witham and the sea.

In the early 17th century, the Rev. John Cotton, vicar of St. Botolph's, and his congregation, played a key role in the founding of Boston, Massachusetts, which was named after the Lincolnshire town. A leading Puritan preacher, Cotton, and many of his followers, moved to the New World in the 1630s, where they largely ran the new settlement for the first half century of its existence.

St. Botolph's Church

THE TALLEST STUMP IN THE LAND

Boston has several other connections with the United States to add to its giving its name to one of that country's major cities. Its first was with the Pilgrim Fathers, a group of Puritans from North Nottinghamshire and Lincolnshire who tried to escape from Britain by boat through Boston. A ship had been organised to take them to the Netherlands, but its captain betrayed the refugees to the local authorities. They were removed from the ship and, according to one of their number, William Bradford, later to become Governor of the Plymouth Colony, *'put into open boats and there rifled and ransacked them, searching them to their shirts for money, yea, even the women further than became modestie'*. They were then taken back to the town and made *'a spectacle and wonder to the multitude, which came flocking on all sides to behould them'*.

The would-be emigrants were taken before the local magistrates and confined to the cells of the Guildhall, but were apparently relatively well treated, and were later able to get away from another part of the Lincolnshire coast. As mentioned earlier, many Bostonians later followed them to the New World, and played a significant part in the establishment of the American Boston and what later became the state of Massachusetts. These contacts ensured a steady flow of visitors from across the Atlantic, and in 1938 an American Room was established in Fydell House, next door to the Guildhall. The room was originally set aside for the use of American visitors to the town, and was formally opened in 1938 by Joseph Kennedy, then US Ambassador to Britain and the father of the late President John F. Kennedy and his brothers. The house was owned by the Fydell family from 1726 to 1868, but is now owned by the Boston Preservation Trust. It serves as an Adult Education centre and the base for a number of groups interested in the history and heritage of the town.

The Guildhall, Boston

THE AMERICAN CONNECTION

Boston Haven, the tidal outlet of the River Witham, was the foundation of the history and prosperity of the town. There may have been a haven, or inlet of the sea, in early times, but it only became significant after the River Witham changed its course, possibly during the floods of 1014, and flowed out through the Haven to the Wash. The increased flow flushed the sediments out of the estuary, allowing ships to approach from the Boston Deeps and come further inland to moor in what became the port of Boston. Trading vessels from Europe were early users of the facilities, allowing the port to become one of the most important, and profitable, in England.

Keeping the approaches clear of mud and silt was always a problem for the port. Falling revenues from trade in the 15th and 16th centuries meant that the work did not get carried out, with the result that access to the wharves was more difficult and trade reduced still further. Fishing remained an important activity, with boats moored well up into the town – as late as the 19th century fish was landed directly into the fish market at the base of the Corporation Buildings between the Market Place and the river.

A new sluice on the Witham in the mid-18th century was designed to speed up the water flow and help scour out the Haven, and the opening of new docks in 1884 allowed shipping to use the facilities regardless of the state of the tides. The docks now handle a steady trade in steel, paper, timber, grain and general merchandise.

A scheme is now in hand to reduce the tidal nature of parts of the haven by building a barrier across the river between the dock entrance and the town. This will allow a tide-free approach to a new lock that has been constructed at the entrance to the South Forty-Foot Drain, part of a plan to provide a through route for pleasure boats from the Witham at Boston to the Nene, and from there into the main inland waterway network.

Boston Haven

A SAFE HAVEN FOR SHIPPING

Draining the Fens was a pretty good job-creation scheme. Initially, men with little more than picks, shovels and aching backs would have put in the hard labour needed to dig the drains, build up the river banks and erect the sea walls. Some would have been locals, particularly at times when farm work was less demanding, but to build defences against the tides you need a lot of hands to build quickly before the work got washed away. Some would have come in from further away, but the work may also have been done by soldiers or prisoners. That 'tradition' continued well into the twentieth century, with German prisoners of war put to work in WWI and Borstal inmates creating their own farm from the sea in the 1930s.

As the defences became more sophisticated, there would also have been a need for men with specialised skills. Carpenters would always have been needed – the thirteenth century Great Sluice at Boston was a timber structure – but brick makers and layers, stone masons and metal workers would all have found jobs building the bridges, locks, sluices and pumping stations that gradually appeared all over the region.

Specialist tools were also needed. Sloughs, ritters, foot irons and tile hooks helped lay field drains and keep ditches clear, while steam-powered drag-line excavators became the machines of choice to clear the bigger waterways.

Modern technology has now replaced many of the jobs and a lot of the old tools and machines, but manpower is still needed by the many Drainage Boards and other agencies who work non-stop to keep our feet dry. Local legend has it that we are all web-footed, but the truth of that is a well-kept Fenland secret.

Sluice Gate

WORK FOR THE WORKERS

The grain harvest has always been one of the key points in the farming year. At one time it would have been the climax of the annual work schedule, and although harvest on the Lincolnshire Fens now continues until much later as the potatoes, beet and vegetables are brought in, there is still a symbolism about having gathered in the wheat, barley, oats and other cereal crops. That significance of Harvest Home is reflected in the celebrations of the Harvest Festival and Harvest Suppers, both of which can be found all over the Lincolnshire Fens.

Harvest Festivals are normally a religious celebration, giving thanks for the gathered crops, and can range from the county-wide service held by the farmers' organisations in the magnificent setting of Lincoln Cathedral to a gathering of friends in the smallest of rural chapels. My grandfather, a Methodist lay preacher, always took the Harvest Festival service at the chapel by Tattershall Bridge, where he gave me my first taste of public speaking by requiring me to read a lesson at the age of about four. My reading wasn't all that good at the time, but he wasn't a chap you argued with over such things. Whatever the size of the congregation, there would always be a fine display of produce in the church ready to be distributed to the poor or needy of the parish.

The poor and needy also benefited from the Harvest Suppers, where a good feed could be had by people who didn't always get the chance to eat well. My mother remembered two such occasions from her childhood in Swaton. One man was seen tucking some left-overs under his cap with the comment, "There's allus tomorrow, yer know", while another asked for "plenty of meeyat", since he got enough potatoes and gravy at home!

A Lincolnshire speciality is the Harvest Supper of our own special dish, stuffed chine. This is a cut from across the shoulders of a pig that has been cured as bacon, with deep cuts in the meat stuffed with parsley before cooking. It is a dish traditionally served at christenings, but is eminently suitable for any special event.

Harvest at Swineshead

HARVEST HOME

38

William Dennis is a classic example of a Fenland farmer who grew from small beginnings. Starting out as a farm worker in the 1850s, he built up a 4,000 acre farming business mainly based on growing potatoes. He was helped by the arrival of railways in the area, which allowed him to sell large tonnages to London and the new industrial cities of the North and Midlands. It is estimated that, in 1904, he sent nearly 2,000 wagonloads from Kirton station alone.

Mr Dennis was a supporter of many charities. He supplied all the potatoes eaten at a dinner in 1901 for the poor of London to mark King Edward VII's coronation, as well as making a gift to the local community of the Kirton Town Hall, a neat little building with a steep roof that looks rather as if it had been transplanted from a small town in France.

Despite a tough business reputation, he was much admired in Kirton. When he lay dying in 1924, straw was spread on the streets outside his home to deaden any noise that might have disturbed him.

After his death, a bronze statue of him was erected outside the Town Hall. Three panels on the pedestal below the statue illustrated what he considered to be his most important activities – growing potatoes, improving wheat yields and draining the land.

One of his farms, Woodlands Farm, is still owned and run as an organic farming enterprise by William's grandson Andrew. Unlike most of the neighbouring farms, which now concentrate on growing crops, Woodlands is run as a mixed farm, with a small herd of Lincoln Red Cattle, a flock of sheep and some traditional Bronze turkeys. The farm also produces vegetables and salads, which are sold through a box scheme to provide affordable organic produce for people living locally. The business also supports a number of arts and community enterprises.

Kirton Town Hall

WILLIAM DENNIS AT KIRTON

The greatest glory of the modern Fens is the magnificent sweep of our big sky. Incomers sometimes feel the very size of it oppressive, especially when the whole dome is obscured by grey clouds or rain, but to those of us who were born here, it lifts the spirits. I lived and worked for several years in Wales, and although the scenery there was often stunning, I missed that openness – the ability to see where you had been and where you were going.

The panoramic setting lends itself well to spectacular visual effects. Sunsets from our western windows can be huge and gaudy, with every colour from the yellow, orange and red end of the spectrum daubed across half the sky. A summer day with light fluffy clouds can be an equal delight for serious spotters or casual dreamers looking for tall towers or graceful galleons, but for weather malevolence there is little that can match a lowering storm bank sweeping in from the east over a landscape still lit by a setting sun low on the opposite horizon. The lightning that cracks down under the storm may be many miles away, and anyone looking for the pot of gold at the end of a rainbow would need to be prepared to travel for it.

Daytime views can be wonderful, but to really appreciate the size and glory of our skies the very best time is a clear and frosty winter's night. Watching for the Geminid meteors in December can be a very cold and sometimes frustrating experience, until you stop looking for the details and just appreciate the stars. Orion stands proud in the south, with the brilliant cluster of the Pleiades to his left and the silver river of the Milky Way flowing right across the heavens. That really is a Big Sky that nothing else can match.

Fosdyke

BIG SKY COUNTRY

Moulton Seas End and Surfleet Seas End share two things in common – they are both called Seas End, and they are both some miles from the sea. Surfleet Seas End is at least close to one of the major Fenland rivers, but Moulton Seas End doesn't even have that maritime connection, so where did the names come from?

The answer, as with so much in the Fens is that what you see now is not what has always been there. Both settlements lie on what was the coast of Lincolnshire until a few hundred years ago, but have found themselves inland as silt built up in the old Bicker Haven, and land was reclaimed from the sea and the marshes. Surfleet Seas End may well have served as the port for the neighbouring larger community of Surfleet, since it is located close to where the Rivers Welland and Glen joined, and where two major drains also emptied into the Welland. That may have meant that it was the highest point to which ships could expect enough depth of water to be able to navigate. The Moulton River, now just a narrow drain, may once have done the same job at Moulton Seas End.

Benington Seas End, just a little way north of Boston, is another stranded coastal community, although the distances there are not as great, and the new land has been created by a combination of long-shore drift of sediments and land reclamation. In the same area, there were plans to establish Frieston Shore as a seaside resort in competition with Skegness, Mablethorpe and others, but while it could still offer the 'bracing' climate that they enjoyed, the mud flats at Frieston did not attract the visitors the way that the sands did at the more successful resorts.

Surfleet Seas End

WHERE DID THE SEAS END?

Spalding is the home of what was probably one of the earliest learned societies in Britain, and certainly the oldest outside London. The Spalding Gentlemen's Society was created in 1710 when a group of local gentlemen, led by Maurice Johnson, then living in Ayscoughfee Hall in the town, got together at a coffee house in Abbey Yard. They discussed local history, studied old books and papers and considered articles in *The Tatler,* a new magazine sent up from London.

What sounds like a rather chatty club was made more formal two years later when *'a Society of Gentlemen, for the supporting of mutual benevolence, and their improvement in the liberal sciences and in polite learning'* was established. Formal meetings took place from that date on, and are still held every Thursday evening throughout the year. To help ensure the maintenance of *'polite learning',* politics and religion are still excluded from the discussions.

Members have included Sir Isaac Newton, Sir Hans Sloane – whose collection became the nucleus of the British Museum, Samuel Wesley, the Lincolnshire-born naturalist Sir Joseph Banks and Alfred Lord Tennyson.

The Society maintains a fine museum in the town, opened on its bicentenary, where the meetings are now held. It also owns an excellent library, with a strong section on the history and antiquities of Lincolnshire. Public lectures are held on a regular basis, covering an esoteric range of topics that have recently included Lincolnshire birds, the Eddystone lighthouse and 'The role of lichens in shaping our world'.

Visits to the Society are encouraged, but membership can only be attained by being nominated by an existing member and being elected by the Council.

Spalding Market Place

THE GENTLEMEN'S SOCIETY

The public house is a vital element in Fenland communities. For many of the scattered locals it was the place to meet, to hear the latest gossip and to pass useful information as to the state of the crops, the prospects for the weather, the state of the tides and the unreasonable demands being made by absent landlords, tithe-hungry churchmen and the drainage courts and commissioners.

The beer that they drank would have either been brewed on the premises, or on a local farm, such as Brewery Farm on Holland Fen, where home-grown barley was malted, fermented in the local water, which offered the additional benefit of purifying it from any unpleasant bugs that might be contaminating it, and delivered to half a dozen pubs within a few miles of the farm.

Many of them also served as hostelries for travellers. The going was often difficult across the Fens and it was unwise, to say the least, to travel far after nightfall, so there needed to be plenty of places that offered a warm fire, a bed and somewhere to get a meal and rest before trudging on through the bogs and woods. Crossroads, junctions and crossing points were good places to set up an inn, so the White Horse, sitting just opposite Spalding's town bridge, and a few yards upstream from the wharves on the River Welland, was in a very good location for travellers, visitors to the town, or merchants with shipping business to deal with.

Sadly, a combination of drink-driving laws, the high price of pub-bought drinks compared to those from supermarkets and the demand by up-market buyers for large houses in remote locations has driven many pubs out of business. The Old Union, which stood at a road junction a few miles from New Bolingbroke, survived for a while as a bikers' pub, but has now gone, as has the Axe and Handsaw at Quadring Eaudyke, the Golden Ball in Holbeach Drove and many others – the Lost Pubs Project lists dozens of them. The Fenland branch of the Campaign for Real Ale – CAMRA – does its valiant best to keep them open, but there is only so much that even so determined a group can do.

White Horse, Spalding

LOCAL RETREATS AND TRAVELLERS' RESTS

One of Spalding's most notable buildings, Ayscoughfee Hall was probably built by Richard Alwyn, a local wool merchant. Tests on some of the old roof timbers show that it was built round about 1450; although later owners have added bits and pieces, as well as removing some that were originally there. The end result is still recognisable in layout and design as one of the best preserved medieval buildings in the country, with a Victorian Gothic frontage and some fine Georgian details inside.

Richard Alwyn's son Nicholas continued to own the house, which is probably mentioned in his will as *my grete house in Spalding*. The same will stated that if neither Nicholas's son nor his nephew had reached the age of 26 the house was to be sold for the benefit of the poor of Spalding, and that sale duly took place. One can only hope that the son and nephew were provided for elsewhere in the will!

A private house for much of its life, the Hall was taken over by the local authority in the early part of the last century and has served as a school, council offices and a library as well as the town museum. It has recently been fully refurbished, and now contains a museum of the house itself as well as of the district of South Holland. There is also an art gallery featuring an ever-changing series of exhibitions. The restoration of the building revealed many secrets of its past, including the fact that the original family wing included two toilets, or garderobes, a very modern feature for its time.

The grounds include formal gardens with a 300 year-old yew walk, a herb garden, an ornamental lake and a more modern Peace Garden. There are also sports facilities and a children's play area.

A project is continuing to find out more about the history of the gardens, with a number of trenches dug in selected locations – though not, the local authority web-site hastily points out, on the bowling green!

School children have been encouraged to help with the excavations, as part of an excellent range of educational opportunities offered in and around the Hall.

Ayscoughfee Hall

SPALDING

The old Fens were a place rich in legends, particularly those that, to give a Fenland twist to the old Scots saying, might be described as ghosties and ghoulies and things that go splash in the night. This was country where you could be lost in seconds as paths petered out in the woods, new bogs could form almost overnight, and streams changed course – or vanished completely, like the ones that once passed under Crowland's Trinity Bridge.

Fogs might last for days, with every stray wisp turning into a ghost or phantom and every ivy-clad tree becoming a troll or a witch waiting to seize the passing traveller. Will o' the wisps danced over the still waters – were they spontaneously igniting methane from the festering depths or were they ghosts following the traveller? Their dark depths could easily be hiding giant eels or monstrous pike, each able to seize a man by the leg and drag him down to a watery doom. There are suggestions that the reason the Danes did not settle in the wetter parts of the Fens was that their own legends were full of flesh-eating demons who lived in swamps, but it seems much more likely that they just preferred to keep their feet dry!

The Fens also shared the common East Anglian belief in Black Dog, an apparition with huge shining eyes. Seeing Black Dog was believed to be a premonition of death, either of the person who saw it, or one of his family, although a more local version, Black Shuck, was sometimes benevolent, leading people, and women in particular, to safety after being lost or in danger.

We had our own local elves, or fairies – the Greencoaties, or Strangers – but we also specialised in Witches and Wise Women. It is as well to know that when the moon itself was trapped in the bogs, and guarded by bogles, boggarts and shapeless Things, the only way that travellers regained its guiding light was by the intervention of a Wise One.

Crowland Bridge

FEN LEGENDS

A ring of great abbeys and monastic houses once encircled the Lincolnshire Fens. Some, like Crowland and Bardney, had been founded in Saxon times. Both were destroyed by invading Danes or Vikings, then rebuilt; Crowland several times over the next three centuries and Bardney in 1087 at the start of a period of expansion that saw over a hundred religious houses established in Lincolnshire, including the Fenland ones such as Kirkstead, Barlings, Swineshead, Revesby, South Kyme, Spalding and Sempringham, the home of the Gilbertines, England's only native religious order.

Many of these establishments became very rich, either by being given or left lands and property or by selling the produce of their lands, with wool being a speciality of many of them. Not all had the highest reputations: according to one old rhyme, the monks at Spalding were *'the gluttons, as all men think'*, and others were reported to take a flexible attitude to vows of poverty or chastity.

Such stories were particularly common during the period before and during Henry VIII's dissolution of the monasteries, and should therefore be taken with at least a pinch of salt, but they may have reduced public opposition to the changes. In Lincolnshire there was a revolt, the Lincolnshire Rising of 1536, although it appears to have been more about the suppression of Catholic worship than the destruction of the religious establishments. Even so, some monks did support the Rising, and suffered the wrath of the King towards our *'Brute and Beastly*

Shire'. Six from Bardney were executed for their role, as was the last Abbot of Kirkstead, Richard Harrison, along with three of his colleagues. Crowland, by contrast, tried to bribe its way out of trouble. It sent a gift of that great Fenland trading commodity, fish, to Thomas Cromwell, Henry's chief minister and keen promoter of the changes, with a note *'ryght mekely besechyng yow lordship favorablye to accepte the same fyshe, and to be gud and favorable lorde unto me and my pore house'*. It did him no good. His *'pore house'* and its great wealth was dispersed along with the others in 1537.

Crowland

THE GREAT ABBEYS OF THE LINCOLNSHIRE FENS

We love our Fenland open landscapes, but when a 'code' east wind comes howling its way across those flat fields, the roads are 'slayap wi iyass' and everything 'clems up', that affection starts to diminish. As a child, my most hated job on the farm was to go out on a winter morning and cut the kale to feed to the cattle. The plants were tall, with a bush of leaves at the top, perfectly designed to hold icy water until this small boy chopped the base of the stem, at which point the whole lot poured down the back of my neck.

Farmers can't afford to be 'nesh' – soft about the weather. Some jobs have to go on. Livestock need to be fed and, if the stockyard troughs or pipes are frozen, watered as well. Any vegetable crops that are accessible need to be harvested and got to market – there might be a premium price for any that make it into the shops.

In the heavy snows of 1947 and 1963 movement almost stopped in many places. Trains couldn't run, snow blocked the roads by piling up into 'reeyaks' – drifts – against any fences or hedges and even the most determined walker would flinch

when he or she realised that the object sticking out of the snow beside them was the top of a telegraph pole.

Snow like that is, fortunately, rare, and what we get

SKATERS AT COWBIT

nowadays is often a source of pleasure, particularly for children released from school, until it thaws. That leaves a residue of 'mud and squad' that bogs down vehicles, 'traipses' into the house and generally depresses everybody. All you can do then is hunker down, grumble at people who won't 'put wudd in th' howall' – shut the door – and wait for spring.

Skating was an important winter sport on the Fens, although milder winters have made it less common today. The Lincolnshire Skating Association held events on Baston Fen until the 1990s, but insurance concerns stopped their activities.

Snow on Cowbit Wash

WINTER ON THE FENS

The industrial archaeology of the Lincolnshire Fens is a fascinating subject. In a landscape almost entirely created by men and machines, the relics of their work can be found in many places in the area. In one sense, the entire environment could be regarded as an industrial artefact, and the study of old drainage patters, the channels that carried water-borne goods to the monasteries from the main waterways and the ways that the soil heaps from salt-making have been incorporated into protective dykes are all the subject of detailed study.

There is also a great pride in the buildings and other structures in the Fens. Some, such as the churches and civic buildings, are still performing the roles they were built for, while others have been modified for new uses, but there are also a considerable number that have been preserved or restored simply because they are right for their localities. Many of them are the result of local volunteer groups who have given time and money to one special project. One suggestion to help with the restoration of Moulton Mill was that a beer would be specially brewed and sold to raise funds. The plan did not go through, although a Moulton Mill beer was created, and can be enjoyed in some pubs in the area.

In other cases, organisations like the Drainage Boards, the people with the most direct responsibility for keeping the Fens the way they are, have cooperated with volunteer groups to allow a facility to be kept in good working order. Two pumping stations on the Lincolnshire Fens show how the land was drained in Victorian times. The Pinchbeck Engine museum, maintained by the Welland and Deepings IDB, includes an original steam-driven beam engine still driving a scoop wheel, while the Dogdyke Pumping Station Preservation Trust maintains what is believed to be the oldest steam-driven scoop wheel pumping set still in operation at its original location.

The Mill, Moulton

LOOKING AFTER OUR HISTORY

As the Fens and marshes were reclaimed, settlements sprang up on the new lands, often miles from their 'parent' village. The distances involved could be too great for parishioners to get to the parish church on a Sunday, so new churches were built, each dedicated to a different saint. The new villages then often took the names of their older counterparts, but with the saint's name added. The bigger villages could acquire quite a number of such satellites, with Holbeach adding St. John's, St. Matthew and St. Mark's, with ten miles separating the furthest flung outposts. Long Sutton saw a similar distance between itself and Sutton St. Edmund, although a traveller between the two would need to pass through Sutton St. James at about the half-way point.

Moulton did not spread quite so far, but Moulton Chapel, a chapel of ease built to make life easier for parishioners at Moulton's own All Saints church, was established five miles south of the main village in 1722 to serve worshippers in that part of the Fen.

The term Chapel could have caused some confusion later on, since it usually applies to the premises of one of the non-conformist groups. The Fens were quite a hot-bed of Methodism in particular, perhaps because of the similarity of the land and people to those in the Isle of Axholme, the Lincolnshire origin of the movement, and home to the Wesley brothers, its founders.

Other outlying communities took more prosaic names – Holbeach and Whaplode Droves marked the end of the paths that animals took to summer grazing, as did Gedney Drove End, while Gedney Dyke and Holbeach Bank sat close to early sea defences.

The Elloe Stone at Moulton Chapel, marks the Moot, or meeting place of the Anglo-Saxons in the south of the Lincolnshire Fens.

Moulton Chapel

TOO FAR TO WALK TO CHURCH

Farms on the Fens would once have been alive with activity as men and women worked to plant, tend and harvest the crops, but it is rare nowadays to see more than one or two people at any given time. Where once there would have been men with scythes or sickles cutting the corn while others gathered it and carted it back to the farmyard, there is now one man on a combine with a couple of other driving grain trailers. The massed gangs of potato planters have been replaced by one machine, and the harvest is again a matter of two or three with big machines. Similarly, the men who pulled a pair of sugar beet roots, banged them together to knock off the soil, sliced off the green tops and threw the roots into a horse-drawn cart have been superseded by a six-row harvester that does everything but turn it into sugar!

My mother talked of a childhood when she and her friends could happily wander the countryside in the knowledge that there would always be a few people in sight singling beet, laying hedges or digging land drains, even when there were no major jobs being done. Those people would know every child and report back about their presence and activities, whereas now we warn children to keep off the fields in case someone in a massive machine fails to notice them, with potentially tragic results.

One farming sector in the Fens has escaped that reduction in workers, and that is the specialist flower and vegetable growing. Some crops have succumbed to total mechanisation, but many still require large gangs of workers, especially at harvest time. No-one has yet developed a machine that can pick just the right buds from a field of daffodils, or that will pick and trim a cauliflower head to leave just the right amount of green leaf protecting the central curd. There may be mechanical assistance, as with the machine seen which carries the trimmed heads to a mobile packhouse, but it still needs men and women with sharp knives to cut and trim the heads.

Vegetable packing, Whaplode

WHERE HAVE ALL THE WORKERS GONE?

The Wash coast near Holbeach is one of the most bombed and rocketed locations in Britain, but is also an important wildlife refuge. The salt marshes and shallow waters of the RAF Holbeach bombing range are used by air forces from Britain, Europe and the United States, but the enforced exclusion of the public allows birds and seals to feed and breed in relative peace. The occasional burst of aircraft fire seems to be much less of a distraction than the people – and their dogs – kept off the area for their own safety.

The range also allows aircraft enthusiasts to practise a hobby popular in Lincolnshire for a century. Known as Bomber County during WWII because of the number of airfields scattered around the county, it has always been important to the Royal Air Force. The Fens themselves were largely free of airfields, partly because the land was too valuable for growing crops, but also because the mists that often cover the landscape made landings and take-offs hazardous, but our big skies made watching aircraft an easy occupation.

My earliest memory is of a sky full of aeroplanes, which my mother tells me was probably the vast fleet of planes and gliders leaving Britain for the attack on Arnhem, but throughout childhood there was the constant hum and splutter of trainee pilots from the RAF College at Cranwell, learning their skills.

There are fewer airfields here now, but Coningsby, on the northern Fens, is still an important base, currently housing our most modern aircraft – the Typhoon fighter – as well as that vital part of our aviation history, the Battle of Britain Memorial Flight. As a child, I would rush out shouting "It's a jet!" when one came over: now it's the sound of Rolls-Royce Merlins driving propellers that gets me out of the house. It may be the Lancaster coming in low heading back to base, or one of the fighters doing lazy circles in the sky as they practice for a demonstration. Either way, it's pure nostalgia.

Mansion House, Holbeach

WILDLIFE UNDER AERIAL ATTACK!

Gedney is probably the epitome of a Lincolnshire Fen landscape. It is so wide and open that even the wind turbines, on their tall towers, seem to get lost in the space, rather than dominating the horizon as they do in more enclosed locations. Crops cling to the ground as if they were afraid that they might soar off into the vastness above them, and the sky itself appears to have an extra dimension with that shimmer, so beloved of children going on holiday, that indicates that the sea is just over the horizon.

The village of Gedney itself is an old settlement, with the -ey ending that shows it was once an island, but Gedney Marsh was nothing but mud and salt flats until 1660, when a new sea wall was built to allow the land behind it to be drained and reclaimed. The top quality Grade 1 silt-based loam soils support a huge range of high value crops; one farmer I know produces hundreds of varieties of salad leaves, while others specialise in flowers, bulbs or potatoes. Until the latter part of the twentieth century it was also famous for its strawberries, but the need for large numbers of hand-pickers, and the inexplicable desire of consumers to eat wooden berries out of season, made it uneconomic, and the trade faded away.

The Gedney area is reputed to be popular with cyclists, who appreciate the level landscape, but it is said that they were only accepted locally when they had completed 'a full Gedney' – riding to each of the six settlements with Gedney in their name, as well as the Marsh and the Fen. The furthest two points lie 16 miles apart, so it is still a challenge, even in the absence of hills.

Daffodils

GEDNEY MARSH

Sir Nikolaus Pevsner, the great recorder of the buildings of England, refers to *'the spectacular architecture'* of the churches in the South Lincolnshire Fens, while the 1911 Encyclopaedia Britannica comments that *'it is principally in the Parts of Holland that the finest churches in the county are found'*. It adds that *'they are not surpassed by those of any other district in the kingdom, which is the more remarkable as the district is composed wholly of marsh land and is without stone of any kind'*.

Standing almost anywhere in the area, it is usually possible to count half a dozen fine spires lifting above the horizon, many of which incorporate materials and architecture going back many hundreds of years. St. Botolph's at Boston is probably the finest single example, but many others attract visitors keen to look into their history. Whaplode, Algakirk and Kirton are all noted by Pevsner as having very early elements in their construction, while St. Mary's at Long Sutton has a fine early 13th century lead-clad wooden spire, which is claimed to be the tallest and oldest in Europe. It also incorporates a fine Norman nave, although the rest of the church has been modified and added to many times over the centuries.

The churches of the fens are often said to have been built on the backs of sheep, since the wool trade with the continent provided much of the medieval wealth of the local communities. The local Lincolnshire Longwool sheep grazed on the marshes and were sheared once a year to yield large fleeces of long-staple wool. The wool was exported to the Continent, usually through the port of Boston, where its hard-wearing properties were much in demand. There are occasional reports that wool bales were used to help firm the foundations of some of the churches, but the value of the product makes that unlikely, although it is possible that a single bale was incorporated under the altar in some places.

St. Mary's, Long Sutton

STONE CHURCHES IN A MUD LANDSCAPE

The two lighthouses that stand on the seaward end of the banks of the River Nene never actually showed a light. They were built by the engineer John Rennie in about 1830 to celebrate the conclusion of the channelling of the river, part of his scheme to improve the local drainage. They were probably intended to carry a lantern on the top-most storey, but they were never added, Rennie having moved on to new projects elsewhere in the country.

Shipping was not left entirely to its own devices, since a customs officer from Sutton Bridge, a few miles up stream, would turn up with a megaphone once a day, just before high tide, to shout instructions to any ship waiting to enter. If he saw no ships, he went home again. A pilot service is now available to shipping, although even that didn't stop one vessel getting stuck across the river a few years ago and having to be scrapped to clear the channel.

In the 1930s, the east tower became the home of the well-known wildlife artist Peter Scott, who used the lantern room as a viewing platform to watch and paint the birds, with the wild geese of the Wash becoming his best-known subjects. According to one story, he came to the area as a keen sporting shot, but gave it up after wounding a goose, and having to watch it die when he couldn't reach it to finish it off.

He left the lighthouse when he joined the Navy at the start of WWII, and did not return to it, but his biographer claimed that he loved it dearly. It is now the starting point for the Peter Scott Walk, a ten-mile stroll along the top of the outer sea bank offering wonderful views of the Wash and the wildlife that uses the salt marshes beyond the defences.

Peter Scott's Lighthouse

SUTTON BRIDGE

Crosskeys Bridge at Sutton Bridge carries the A17 road linking South Lincolnshire with Norfolk and the East Anglian ports. The fruit and vegetable traffic was once described as *'a river of onions flowing north, while brussel sprouts headed south'*. The bridge is the third to cross the Nene at this point and, like its predecessors, had to be able to open to let shipping reach the port of Wisbech.

The first structure was designed by the great road and canal engineer John Rennie, and was built of oak, with a movable section made of cast iron. It was welcomed by contemporaries although, as one pointed out, it just made it easier to get from one set of *'treacherous tidal sands'* to another, since the town of Sutton Bridge only sprang up after the bridge was opened.

The second bridge had an equally famous designer in Robert Stephenson. The Lynn and Sutton Bridge Railway Company later modified it by laying rails alongside the roadway, but the structure proved inadequate for the traffic. It was replaced in 1897 by the current structure, built by the L&SB's successor, the Midland and Great Northern Railway Company.

The M&GN, which ran from the East Midlands to the Norfolk coast, carried two main traffics, fruit and vegetables from the Fens and holidaymakers to the seaside. The bridge still carries both, al-though they now travel by road, with much grumbling whenever the narrow lanes, a loaded lorry or a passing ship slows their dash to their destinations. The closing of the railway is often blamed on the infamous Dr Beeching, but the end came for trains over Crosskeys Bridge in February 1959, well before he had even been commissioned to write his report. Ironically, the final day was one of the busiest for years, with nine trains of football fans crossing the bridge on their way home to Sheffield from Norwich.

Recent road improvements led to suggestions that the bridge should be replaced, but this historic structure has survived, complete with its iconic signal box on top of the girders. The bridge is now swung by electric motors, but the original hydraulic cylinders and piping have been preserved in a private dwelling on the north bank of the river.

The Toll House that stands guard at the end of the bridge collected the tolls for passage over one of the earlier structures, then part of an improved dryland route created as the marshes between Lincolnshire and King's Lynn in Norfolk were reclaimed for farming.

Crosskeys Bridge

AND ITS RAILWAYS, SUTTON BRIDGE

A Fens Miscellany

To understand how the Fens were formed, a good start would be to dig a hole. It would need to be a deep hole, and it might be a good idea if you grew some gills, because the pit would fill with water pretty quickly. As you dug, you'd find layers of silt, gravel, peat and clays that go back thousands of years, into the Ice Ages, eventually arriving at a thick bed of much older clay that forms the underlying structure.

Geologically, the whole Fen area, including those parts beyond the county boundary in Norfolk and Cambridgeshire, lies in a great bowl of that clay, laid down 150 million years ago in the Jurassic period. At that time, dinosaurs roamed the Earth and Britain was at about the latitude of present day Spain, lying under a warm shallow sea in which fine sediments were deposited as beds of clay. This was later covered by chalks and limestone, but over the Fens they were eroded away to leave the clay base. During the Ice Ages, as the ice sheets came and went, rivers and the sea deposited layers of silt and clay, with the relative proportions changing with sea level. Daniel Defoe, writing in the early 18th century, described the whole area as a 'soak' into which 'the waters of thirteen counties' drained. Finally, over the past 20,000 years, since the last Ice Age, the growth of vegetation, followed by later flooding, has left large areas of peat. The origin of the peat can be very obvious when a plough hits what are called bog oaks – large pieces of tree trunk that have almost been fossilised in the soil. Such a collision can be very expensive for the farmer concerned, but it is a risk that most of them have been happy to take, since the peat soils are among the finest in the world for agricultural production.

The area is not quite as flat as it sometimes seems: the whole area is known as Holland, not because of the similarity to the Netherlands but from old words for the 'high land' between the Fens and the sea. A long bank of silt just inland of the present coast provided the drier ground for a line of villages north-east of Boston, continuing along the old sea coast through Kirton and Sutterton before turning north to Donington along the shore of what was then Bicker Haven. A similar low ridge, or line of islands, laid the foundations for the settlements from Long Sutton through Holbeach to the Moultons. More villages mark the divide of the East Fen from the West and Wildmoor Fens, occupying a series of islands along a glacial moraine – a heap of clay and stony rubble – left after the last Ice Age. Sibsey and Stickney still retain the ending –*ey*, meaning an island.

The earliest land reclamation projects in the area were probably the construction of sea banks to help protect the villages from high tides and storms. We now call most of them Roman Banks, but whether the Romans actually constructed them is not something that archaeologists and historians agree on. They certainly did use parts of the Fens, since a number of settlements can be found along the edges, linked by their long, straight roads. While driving round the county, I can't help but think that the last time Lincolnshire had a modern road system was 2,000 years ago, since we still use the same main routes as the legions would have marched on! They built Ermine Street and King Street to the west of the Fens, as well as the route from Lincoln round the northern edge which

may have led to a port at or near Wainfleet or, according to one intriguing theory, a lost Roman town on the coast near Skegness.

Farming appears to have been quite extensive on the Fens themselves in Roman times. The archaeological traces of buildings, field boundaries and small communities can be detected quite easily in aerial photographs, although there is little evidence for larger brick or stone buildings. Nearly all such remains are covered with marine deposits, which suggests that major flooding by the sea took place after Roman times, leading some experts to argue that any defences that the Romans built would have been washed away by the waters. Alternatively, new defences may have been built in response to the rising tides, either by later Romano-British inhabitants, or by the Anglo-Saxons who followed them onto the Fens.

Whoever it was who built the banks, they did it well. Those structures have been the foundation for almost all the reclamation schemes that have followed.

The impact of the incoming Anglo-Saxons is most apparent in the village names along the drier land close to the coasts. The ending –*ton* can mean an enclosed village or farmstead, and appears in Bennington, Wibberton, Frampton, Kirton, Gosberton, Donington, Moulton and the Suttons, among others. Add in the –*eys*, –*wicks* and –*ings* and you could be drawing up a glossary of local place names, although the suffixes can sometimes mislead – what would seem to be the most obvious example, Boston, only came into prominence in the 11th century.

The other major community in the modern Lincolnshire Fenland, Spalding, was certainly established by this time, probably on the combination of quality silt land and the lowest crossing point of the Welland. It may have been founded in about 600 by a group known from other sources as the Spalda, although there is always the possibility that a community already existed there, but was renamed by the incomers.

Over the second half of the first millennium, new settlers gradually moved in to the Fens, often arriving first as raiders, but returning later to establish new homes. The Danish influence is very strong in Lincolnshire, which has more names ending in the characteristic suffix –by than any other county, although there are fewer of them in the lower-lying lands. Wigtoft, Brothertoft and Fishtoft may well be Danish, but could also be linked to the next major influence in the area – the Vikings, who followed the same pattern of pillaging first and settling later.

One other group of 'settlers' were the religious communities which developed on the Fen edges at places like Bardney, Partney and Crowland, setting a pattern that was to hold un-

til the dissolution of the monasteries by Henry VIII. These communities were among the first to systematically set out to improve the agriculture in their localities, and became rich on the proceeds. Unfortunately, that affluence made them attractive targets for each successive wave of raiders, and most were sacked and burned several times in the first couple of centuries of their existence.

The great majority of this settlement took place on the higher lands, but most of the Fens themselves, along with the coastal marshes, were not attractive to the newcomers. Drier stretches would have allowed for some farming, but summer grazing for livestock was the main agricultural activity.

That doesn't mean that the Fens were not valued by the local inhabitants. To some observers it was *a hideous fen of huge bigness… oft-times clouded with moist and dark vapours*, in which could be found *strange and uncouth monsters*, who, according to St. Guthlac's biographer,

'were cruel, and of form terrible, having great heads,
long necks, lean faces, pale countenances, ill-favoured
beards, rough ears, wrinkled foreheads, stinking mouths,
teeth like horses, spitting fire out of their throats',

who threw the saint into *the dirty fen*. I do remember people like that from my childhood, but most were somewhat better looking, although they might well have been keen to lob the odd self-professed holy man into the nearest swamp!

The alternative view, as propounded by William of Malmesbury, was that they were,

> *'a very paradise and a heaven for the beauty there-of ... there is such abundance of fish as to cause as-tonishment to strangers, while natives laugh at their surprise. Water-fowl are so plentiful that per-sons may not only assuage their hunger with both sorts of food, but can eat to satisfy for a penny'.*

Eels were so plentiful in the Fens that, in addition to serving as food and medicinal aids, they were almost a local currency. Rents, debts, church tithes and other dues were often settled in eels. The numbers could be huge – one monastery received 60,000 eels a year from 20 fishermen as rent for the fishery. The mind boggles at the thought of trying to deal with that many live eels – Fen fisherman will tell you that dealing with one is hard enough – but other records show payments of hundreds of barrels of eels, presumably caught and salted to preserve them for future use.

The Fens did not just offer fish and fowl to the locals. They also provided fuel in the form of wood, charcoal and peat; a wide range of fruits and berries and a commodity that could be highly valued in turbulent times – security. The best known exponent of the latter is probably Hereward the Wake, a land-owner from Bourne, another of my childhood heroes, who took to the Fens to conduct what we would now describe as guerrilla warfare with William the Conqueror following the Norman invasion. On the downside, Fen 'slodgers' may have had to put up with 'Fen ague', possibly a form of malaria. A possible source of 'Yellerbelly' is that opium was grown to treat the ague, and the skins of regular users could develop a yellow-ish, jaundiced look.

The Norman Conquest concentrated land holdings in the Fens into the hands of Norman landlords and the Church, and both continued reclaiming small areas of land outside the existing banks, or improving the drainage of fields within them. The Abbot of Crowland is credited with 'improving' the marshes round his Abbey, allowing the monks to grow more grain there, while a Norman *'man much addicted to agricul-ture'*, Richard de Rulos, reclaimed land round the Deepings as *'meadow and pasture'*.

Villagers also participated. The common land along the silts from Spalding to Moulton was drained and divided up among the local inhabitants, who, it was reported, used the *'rich and fruitful earth'* for arable crops, pasture or hay-making.

Where streams or drains passed through the 'Roman' banks they were usually protected by sluices – gates which allowed water to flow out at low tides, but closed against an inflow when the waters outside were higher than those within. A much larger sluice was erected in the middle 12th century on the Witham at Boston, by then its main outlet to the sea, both to protect against high tides and also to *increase the rush and force of the waters, by which the harbour is made clear*.

Clearing the channel was vital, because Boston was well on its way to becoming one of the most important ports in England. At the end of the 12th century, it was second only to London in the harbour dues collected there, and it overtook the capital in the following century, reaching the height of its importance in the late 1300s, when it held the wool staple – the right to collect taxes on all wool leaving the country.

Despite the improvements in the drainage, the Fens continued to be inundated at frequent intervals. In the great flood of 1287 the area was,

for the most part turned into a standing pool, so that an intolerable multitude of men, women and children were overwhelmed with the water, especially in the town of Boston, a great part of which was destroyed.

A number of commissions were set up to consider how the situation might be improved and one, in the reign of James I, proposed action, but Parliament threw out the taxes to pay for it. Some things never change....

Some action was being taken by individual landowners or small groups. The Hobhole and Maud Foster Drains were cut in the 1580s to help drain the land north of Boston. A large area of marsh between the Welland and the Nene outfalls was enclosed in 1615 by a group of adventurers led by the Duke of Argyll, and powers to do the same were offered for the Sutton marsh, the Fens east of Bourne and Sleaford and the whole of the Witham Fens running north-west from the Kyme to Lincoln.

Some of these schemes were carried out while others vanished without a trace of spade being dug into soil, but wherever they took place, they met with strong opposition from the local Fen Tigers. The English Civil War, in particular, gave them an opportunity to destroy the dykes, fill in the drains and reverse the sluices. All such projects had been promoted in the name of the King, who normally retained a fifth of any new land created, a fact which Cromwell ensured was widely known.

There is no doubt that a well-ordered way of life was under threat. The Fen Code, a list of rights and responsibilities, had been drawn up in the middle of the 16th century. No per-sons without commoners' rights were to pasture any cattle, catch fish or fowl, cut turves or collect fodder unless authorised by a commoner. Cattle were not to be moved at night or on Sundays, reeds had to be at least two years old before they could be cut for thatch, and all livestock on the common fen had to be marked as to who owned them. As a small-scale farmer afflicted by modern rules and paperwork, I can sympathise with the irritation they may have felt, but it did ensure that life was relatively ordered despite being lived in a very disordered place.

An uneasy peace reigned on the Fens following the restoration of the Monarchy, although there were still outbreaks of public opposition. In 1699, a large crowd from South Holland wrecked drainage works *under colour and pretence of foot ball playing*. Football hooliganism is obviously not as new as we thought it was. However, the onward march of enclosure, where common land was divided up between the individual farmers, and a new enthusiasm for draining rapidly overwhelmed any local opposition.

A Bill was passed in Parliament in 1762 which allowed for the straightening of the Witham and the improvement of the low lands on either side of it. It was soon followed by similar treatment of the Black Sluice district, drained by the South Forty Foot; Deeping Fen and the East and West Fens. The legislation was all in place by 1801. The modern South

Lincolnshire Fens were about to be born, but one problem still had to be solved.

That was something that had not been encountered by the Dutch drainers on whose experience the English engineers had depended. The peat soils in the Fens shrank by a combination of drying out, wind erosion and the oxidation of the exposed surface. Drains that had run to the sea by gravity were now below sea level, and pumping had to be used to lift the water high enough to escape. Wind power was the first method, with great scoop wheels turned by the power of the sails lifting the water up into higher level drains. The windmills were gradually replaced, first by steam engines – still driving scoop wheels – then by diesels driving centrifugal pumps. The modern power source of choice is electricity, although many diesel pumps are still kept on standby in case of power failures or extra demand. There are still a few steam engines to be seen, but they are mainly run by volunteers, just some of the many keepers of the heritage of the Fens.

RIVERS AND DRAINS

Visitors to our house on the banks of the Witham often ask about 'the canal', rather than the river. It's an understandable mistake, because, like most of the Fenland waterways, it is relatively straight and enclosed in high artificial banks, so doesn't look much like the rivers of most people's imaginations. A few hundred years ago, they all looked much more like natural rivers. The Witham rises in south Lincolnshire, west of the Heath, and runs north before turning sharply east through the Lincoln Gap. Below the Gap it weaved and curled its way south across the lowlands, picking up the waters of the Barlings Eau, the Bain and the Slea at varying points along its wandering route. The Nene, once known as the Wellstream, constantly changed its outlet into the Wash – the current county boundary with Norfolk follows an old route of the stream, rather than the apparently obvious modern boundary marked by the modern course.

The Welland and the Glen would both have emptied into the old Bicker Haven, but the large deposits of silt around what would have been their mouths suggest that they too switched courses often over the years. There is a suggestion that the names Welland and Glen are derived from old words for 'muddy' and 'clean' since the Welland carried reddish sand and silt from the easily eroded ironstone beds in Northamptonshire, while the Glen came down quickly from the limestone uplands of the Lincolnshire Heath. Its headwaters lie only a mile or two from those of the Witham.

All the rivers are now channelled and serve mainly as routes to the sea for the upland waters from beyond the Fens. The same applies to the 'Delphs' that flow eastwards across the Witham Fens, carrying water to the river from the uplands to the west, and the long Maud Foster Drain, one of the earliest of the major Lincolnshire Fen drainage works, which flows straight to the sea from the foothills of the Wolds.

Most of the waters from the Fens themselves are carried on the great drains that were dug between the 16th and 18th centuries. The North and South Forty Foot Drains now take most of the water from the western Witham Fens, the Hobhole takes it away from the East and West Fens, the North and South Counter drains clear the land between the Welland and the Glen and the South Holland Main Drain is, logically enough, the main drain in South Holland.

Feeding into the main drains are a host of smaller waterways – a combination of natural streams, such as the Whaplode River and the Hammond Beck; early partial drainage schemes like the Black Dyke, Vernatt's Drain and the South Ea and newer cuts made to link straight into the larger courses. These would include most of the waterways in the East Fen and the Black Sluice District to the east of Bourne. A modern map of the works controlled by any of the South Lincolnshire Drainage Boards is now an astonishing complex of lines often going right down to the ditches between the fields. Even that level of detail is not the final stage, since it would be possible to continue to a further scale – usually only of interest to the individual farmer – the underground clay or plastic pipes that have been laid by him or his predecessors to ensure that the soil itself does not become saturated. Water, and its movements, is a vital concern to every Fenlander, so it is just as well that we are well cared for by the Drainage Boards, without whom we would soon be in a very sorry – and wet! – state.

WHERE TO NOW FOR THE SOUTH LINCOLNSHIRE FENS?

The story of the South Lincolnshire Fens may seem to be finished, but drainage never stops, and the constant erosion of some of the best soils is reducing the agricultural value of substantial areas.

In some places, the waters are already returning to cover the land, or at least to make it much wetter. Coastal defences have been abandoned or realigned at several locations to permit protection to be maintained more conveniently or at a lower cost. Some of those schemes, such as that at Frieston Shore adjacent to the North Sea Camp prison farm, have also become valuable nature reserves, restoring some of the coastal habitats that have been lost to reclamation.

There are also purely conservation projects like that at Willow Farm, Tongue End, where nearly 300 acres of farmland are to be allowed to revert to fen, thereby linking two existing smaller fenland reserves at Thurlby and Baston. The land has been bought by the Lincolnshire Wildlife Trust, with the aid of a grant from the National Lottery. The chief executive of the Trust described the purchase as *'a great opportunity to redress the balance',* following the loss of over 99.9% of the inland fen landscape to drainage schemes. Once the landscape there has been restored, the arable fields will become a diverse and wildlife-rich landscape of shallow pools, reedbeds and grazing marshes. Rare fenland species, including aquatic plants, insects, fish and birds will be able to spread out into the new, larger area.

To some farmers, any such reversion seems almost criminal. They see a world where food is getting scarcer and more expensive, and argue that land as good as that in the Fens should be used intensively for food production, with conservation reserved for lower quality areas.

Longer term, it may be that a combination of rising sea levels and potential climate change will mean that many of the assumptions of the farmers, drainers and conservationists all have to be questioned. It would seem inconceivable that such a valuable resource as the South Lincolnshire Fen farmland could ever be surrendered, but nothing is impossible in these changing times.

BOSTON: THE MOST FAMOUS TOWN IN LINCOLNSHIRE?

It may have come as a surprise to Lincoln, and possibly Grimsby and Grantham as well, that that chronicler of *The Kings England,* Arthur Mee, should claim that *'in all Lincolnshire there is no town more famous'* than Boston. Mee may have been being disingenuous in that Lincoln is a city rather than a town, so he could exclude it from consideration, but he was probably considering the port's rich history, and the way that it still exhibits so much of that past.

On the face of it, Boston is just another medium-sized country town with a fine market place and a tall church – you can't miss it; you've been looking at it for miles regardless of the direction you came from! A glimpse of cranes over the rooftops show it is also a port, but that about concludes the first impression. However, once you get into the town the history becomes more apparent. The river is the key since that determined its location. It can be anything from a small stream flowing between mud banks to a brown torrent depending on the state of the tides and the rainfall over about half of Lincolnshire.

Boston does not appear in the Domesday Book, although Fishtoft and Skirbeck, now parts of the town, do. The town probably grew after the Witham adopted a new course through it some time in the eleventh century.

The new town offered a sheltered harbour ideally situated for trade with the continent, and the junction of land routes across the Fens made it a good place for trading with the locals. The first market charter was granted to Boston in 1204 and an annual fair under the charter took place less than twenty years later, although fairs had been held in the town since the 1120s. Boston still has an excellent annual fair, but with more swing-boats than horse-traders.

The thirteenth century was a busy time. The Barditch, with its associated earth bank, was dug on the eastern side, probably as a defensive structure, but also marking the boundary of the town. A bridge was built over the Witham, possibly where a set of sluice gates controlled the river waters. Several sets of friars took up residence, and the Guild of The Blessed Virgin Mary was formed. The port was also thriving, with nearly a third of English wool exports leaving through the docks and large volumes of wine, timber and other commodities coming in. It became a port of the Hanseatic League, an organisation of merchants trading in the Baltic Sea and around Northern Europe. By the end of the century, the town was collecting more customs dues than any other port in the Kingdom.

The expansion continued into the fourteenth century, with the building between 1309 and 1390 of the main body of St. Botolph's Church, the setting up of more Guilds and the granting to the port of the wool staple, which restricted the trading of wool, and the collection of taxes on it, to a small number of locations. All this, despite several outbreaks of the Black Death, one of which, legend has it, was brought to the town by a visiting young man indulging in a close personal relationship with the wife of a local merchant.

That first Boston would have been built of wood, not the longest lasting of building materials, and a major fire in 1281 ensured that anything that might have survived to the present day vanished overnight, but the layout of the town is still clear from the modern street patterns. Stroll along the east of the Market Place, and you will see a number of snickets – narrow alleyways – running between many of the buildings. The buildings occupy narrow plots that extend well to the rear, and would have reached back to the Barditch, into which was dumped noisome refuse, just the kind of thing that really excites an archaeologist.

South Street includes the Guildhall of St. Mary, once thought to date from the fifteenth century, but now recognised as including elements of a building constructed in the 1390s. The spectacular black and white building close to it, Shodfriars Hall, has been reconstructed several times in its history, but the original foundation probably dates back to the fourteenth century, as does the Blackfriars Theatre, down Spain Lane, once the refectory for the friars. Sitting rather forlornly in a retail development is Pescod Hall, another fifteenth century building which was moved in its entirety from its original location. Once a high-grade merchant's house, it is now a fast-food outlet.

St. Botolph's church is the most significant survivor of those days, although the tower – the Stump – itself dates from a hundred years later. The misericords in the stalls display a wonderful selection of carvings dating from the times, including mythical beasts, flowers and heraldic designs as well as some very ordinary scenes, including a schoolboy trying to protect himself with a book while being caned. Anyone trying that in my schooldays just had the number of strokes doubled!

North of the church, Wormgate still follows the winding route of a street backing onto the river, and Wide and Strait Bargate, the main commercial streets of the town, run from the Market Place towards the town perimeter. Just to confuse the issue, –*gate* in this context is likely to mean street, rather than gate, so Bargate probably means Gate Street.

The next couple of hundred years were not so kind to Boston. The wool trade became less important, the river began to silt up, making it harder for ships to get into the port, and the Hanseatic merchants stopped using the port. In the mid-fifteenth century Henry VIII closed all the friaries, although he established Boston as a borough in 1455, allowing the town two Members of Parliament.

Initially, the loss of trade did not seem to hurt the town in general. A great house was built in about 1450 for Sir Richard Benington, the collector of customs duties, who must have managed to pocket a few for himself since the house included a great hall, gatehouse and servants quarters, as well as a tower, one of the earliest buildings in Lincolnshire to be built entirely of brick. All that is left now is that tower, known as the Hussey Tower, after a later owner of the house. Lord Hussey was executed for treason by Henry VIII, and the tower eventually passed into the ownership of the Corporation. They cannot be said to have looked after it, since it is now a sad relic of its former grandeur.

The Stump tower was completed in about 1515 and Boston Grammar school founded in 1555. Its library, built in 1567, can still be seen in the town. The Maud Foster Drain was dug in the mid-sixteenth century, an early indication of a future role as one of the main centres of the drained Fenland.

Boston next came to prominence in 1607, when a group of religious dissidents from the Gainsborough area tried to escape illegally on board a ship to the Netherlands. The captain of the ship betrayed them and the story has it that they were imprisoned in the cells beneath the Guildhall, serving at that time as the local town hall. This has ensured a valuable import trade to the town of American visitors, since the dissidents later escaped by way of the Humber and are now better known as the Pilgrim Fathers. Boston, a strongly Puritan town, continued to supply the American colonies with a steady flow of emigrants as well as the name for one of their major cities.

Prosperity gradually returned to Boston as the Fens were drained and the trade in farm products became more important. The current Grand Sluice was erected on the Witham in 1766, although one visitor was less than impressed by the hospitality following the opening. He wrote:

Boston, Boston, Boston, thou hast nought to boast on
But a Grand Sluice and a High Steeple
A proud, conceited, ignorant people
And a coast where souls get lost on.

Many of the civic buildings in Boston date from around this time. A new Customs House was built in 1725, and Fydell House, next door to the Guildhall, was constructed the following year for William Fydell, a 3-times mayor of the town. An American room was dedicated there in 1938 by Joe Kennedy, President John Kennedy's father. The Corporation Buildings between the market and the river had a fish market on the ground floor served from the quays behind. The occupants of the upper floors must have had to get used to the smell of fish, particularly in the summer months.

The fine Maud Foster windmill was built in 1819, and still offers flour for sale. The Assembly Rooms on the Market Place were opened three years later. The Great Northern Railway and the East Lincolnshire Railways converged on the town in 1848 and although Dr Beeching savaged the lines into the town, trains still run and the station architecture continues to be appreciated. New docks were opened in 1884, which reduced the inconvenience of having to deal with tides while loading or unloading, and although the fishing fleet is now only a shadow of its former self, boats still moor alongside the river quays.

The twentieth century saw two new bridges over the Witham – or three if you count the attractive footbridge from the police station to the Market Place; very useful on a Saturday night – a rather ostentatious Centenary Methodist Chapel, the Central Park of my childhood memories and new roles for the Guildhall. In 1929 it became the Town Museum, which has recently been nicely upgraded, but during WWII it served as a British Restaurant. I have a copy of a lovely piece of film showing locals dining on their one shilling (5p) lunches under the not very approving stares of the portraits of local dignitaries. The original guild, which apparently once spent the equivalent of £10,000 on a banquet, would probably have been shocked!

Boston today is a busy market town, desperate for a by-pass to get some of the traffic off its narrow streets, where you can now hear more languages than have been heard since the great days of the Hanseatic League. Just like in those times, the various nationalities that live and work around Boston fall out with each other, but also as in those times, the trading opportunities offered by the incomers makes for a more interesting shopping experience. Produce from Poland, Russia, Portugal, the Far East and the Arab world are all on offer in Boston, which means that a day exploring this old Fenland town can be rounded off with an interesting meal. Sounds a good combination to me!

SPALDING: THE FOOD HUB OF BRITAIN

Spalding, with its surrounding district of South Holland, has been described as 'the Food Hub of Britain'. That's a pretty accurate description: according to the National Centre for Food Manufacturing, based in Holbeach, twenty percent of all Britain's foodstuff passes through the district, which not only produces large numbers of crops, it also imports, processes, packs and distributes them all over the country.

Look around you almost anywhere in the area, at any time of the year, and it will be obvious where much of that produce is coming from. Harvesting will be going on to gather in one or more of the many crops for which the area is famous. Mainstream produce such as grain, potatoes and sugar beet all have their own seasons, with massive machines to do most of the work, but the flowers, salads and vegetables tend to be gathered in all year round, and their variety and value means that many of them are still picked by hand. The sight of a gang stripped for action in mid-summer can make the job seem quite inviting, but the same team, clothed down in boots, gloves and as many layers of clothes that they can cram on, picking brussel sprouts on a freezing January morning will soon dispel any such romantic notions.

Much of the land now being cropped would have been too wet to farm in the past, although there is some evidence that Spalding served as a Roman port. At that time the Fens were drier and more suited to arable farming than they became in the Middle Ages, so food may well have been exported from there. That key dietary requirement, and vital tool for the preservation of food – salt – was also produced in the area from very early times. The remains of pre-Roman and Roman saltings have been found at Spalding, Cowbit and Holbeach and the chemical would have been sent elsewhere in Britain as part of a Roman soldier's salarium or salt supply.

Spalding also had a very early market – it is one of the few towns recorded as having one in the Domesday Book. The Priory in the town had its own herring fleet, as well as being famous for the quantity of wool produced by the flocks which grazed on the neighbouring marshes. In 1586 William Camden seemed to be surprised to find it to be *'a fairer towne … than a man would looke to find in this tract among such slabbes and water-plashes…'.*

Food 'exports' from South Holland before drainage took place would probably have been limited to the eels mentioned earlier and wild fowl trapped in decoys – ponds laid out with netted tunnels leading off into which the birds could be driven or enticed. The monks of Crowland Abbey seem to have been the first to use decoys in Britain, but since decoy is derived from the Dutch for duck trap they probably imported the idea from there.

Sheep were the main farm animals found on the Fens, but they were mainly kept for wool. There was strong demand for English wool by continental merchants, and the Lincolnshire Fens and marshes were well suited to 'finishing' the sheep – growing it to its full size and maximum wool cover. Many of the great Fenland churches, including Boston's magnificent 'Stump', are said to have been built on the backs of sheep – paid for by the wool trade. No chance of that nowadays; it costs more to shear a sheep than the wool is worth!

Mutton was a less important by-product. Farm workers right up to the 20th century grumbled with good reason at having to eat the meat from sheep that were too old to produce a good crop of wool. Boiling for some hours was the recommended cooking method, but the result could still be too tough for men who often had few teeth to chew it with.

Cattle from northern England and Scotland were driven south to the Fens to fatten up in the summer before continuing their journey towards the markets in London, but the local diet was more likely to be supplemented by meat from a pig fed on scraps and whatever it could root up for itself around the farms and villages. The whole county still has a long and proud tradition of using 'everything but the grunt' that comes from a pig. Companies such as George Adams, based in Spalding, turned that tradition into a business, and their pork products can still be found in shops all over the country.

Arable cropping in the early days consisted mainly of barley, which grew better on the salty silt soils that wheat or oats, with some beans, flax for fabric production and possibly some woad for dying cloth.

As land was reclaimed a greater variety of crops began to be grown, with oats and oilseed rape being added, along with some fruit, particularly in and around Donington and Holbeach, but the real boost to food production came with the railways, which allowed fresh produce to get to the markets in good condition.

Potatoes became one of the most important crops, as shown by the old rhyme:

When at last the fenman dies, and comes to Heaven's gates
He'll ask the angel at the door 'Now, what's the price of tates?

They are still a key part of the local farming, although infes-tations of nematode worms, encouraged by growing the crops too frequently on the same land, have made production on the silts less profitable.

Cabbages, cauliflowers, broccoli, carrots, peas, brussel sprouts, salad leaves and onions were soon added, laying the foundations for today's field vegetable crop sector, with a large proportion of the whole national crop of many of them now being grown in the area. Farmer cooperatives sprang up in many locations to coordinate production and try to build a position of strength to deal with the big retail groups, but most of them have now been converted into more conventional commercial businesses.

Some specialist crops thrived for a while, but then declined in the face of competition from other areas. Strawberries were grown in large numbers around Long Sutton, fruit trees and bushes became popular, and peppermint oil was produced from crops grown around Holbeach, but they all eventually lost out to lower cost producers in the UK or overseas. Black fen celery is still the best there is, but a recent attempt to re-start the market failed, possibly because modern consumers disliked the small amounts of black soil to be found between the stems. Another farmer told me that his father had grown opium poppies in the years after WWII, and that the odd plant still turned up every now and then in his garden. I don't think it was an excuse in case the Drugs Squad dropped in.

Sugar beet is still important, although the factory at Spalding closed some years ago, and local growers now take their crop to Norfolk for processing.

All that food was way beyond the ability of local or even national markets to consume it all on a seasonal basis, so companies such as Smedleys and Lockwoods began processing and canning crops such as carrots and peas, but the big growth in that sector has been the demand by modern supermarkets for products to be prepared and packed ready for sale. The pack-houses that do this for them now also import the crops from overseas to ensure the year-round supply of products. Keen followers of one supermarket or another would be surprised, and possibly a little put out, to see identical produce going into similar packs with different labels on them, sometimes at very different prices! Chilled ready meals are also prepared and packed, and the competition between growers and packers to think up new products or ideas is very keen.

Crop picking and packing would once have been done by gangs of local women and children, or by groups of travelling Irishmen, who were housed in barns or sheds known locally as 'Paddy houses'. Gypsies and other travellers were common in the strawberry fields, and in WWII German and Italian prisoners were used. My aunt, who worked on the land with them, suggested that the Italians were more interested in chatting up the local girls than picking the crops, which resulted in

'the odd scrap' on a Saturday night. Nowadays seasonal workers often come into the area from Eastern Europe or Portugal, but they are only following in a long-established tradition, including the chatting up and the scraps!

The Flowering Fens

As a child in the 1950s a spring treat would be to be taken for a drive through the bulb fields around Spalding. The memory of the gaudy colours of those tulips in full bloom still remains with me as the epitome of how a garden should look, much to the despair of my wife, who prefers less showy plants, ideally with a longer flowering season!

Bulbs have been grown there for well over a hundred years. The first crops were snowdrops grown for medicinal purposes, although the flowers were also sold through the London markets. Shortly before the beginning of the 20th century daffodils were added and tulips came in a few years later, influenced by a number of Dutch growers who came to South Holland. Cornelius Slooten, van Konynenburg, and the van Geest brothers all helped the locals get used to wrapping their tongues around unusual foreign names.

By the 1930s it was a big business: hundreds of tons of flowers left Spalding and other local railway stations on their way to the markets. Unlike today, when they are shipped out as buds, they were usually sent in full flower; homes in those days had no central heating so the blooms didn't die off as fast as they do now. The industry also helped in the WWII war effort, when four million flower bulbs were sent to America to help pay for those war-time essentials, 'guns and butter'.

The gorgeous colours in the fields caused chaos before the war when, following big publicity for a very patriotic display of colours to celebrate King George V's Jubilee of 1935, vast numbers of trippers in buses, charabancs and any other vehicle that could be pressed into service, jammed all the little local roads with sightseers. WWII stopped the havoc, but growers and the RAC got together after the war to designate a formal route to be followed during a designated Tulip Week. An even better solution was devised in the late 1950s.

All the spring flowers were grown for their bulbs as well as the blooms, but to get good-sized bulbs it was essential that the heads be removed. Some went as flowers but the rest were discarded which resulted in South Lincolnshire having what must have been the most colourful rubbish tips in the world. It also resulted in some disappointed flower tourists who found fields of green stalks where they had expected bands of brilliant colours.

To solve the problem, local growers borrowed an idea from the Dutch and used the discarded heads to decorate floats to be used in an annual Flower Parade through Spalding. A steel framework is built onto a lorry, trailer or any other movable vehicle, the framework is covered, originally with straw matting, but now with plastic foam sheet, and the heads are pinned onto the matting by volunteers working flat out, often day and night, to get the floats finished in the two days before the Parade – any earlier and the heads would have gone limp and drab before the event.

The scenes in the sheds where the floats are fitted out are a fantastic buzz of colour and action. I've watched the whole process a number of times, and the skill and enthusiasm of the workers is a delight to see, although the air has been known to turn blue on occasion when a pin finds a finger rather than the base covering. It's a pity they can't catch the colour, since there are no real blue tulips, which limits the colour palette of the designer.

The Parade day itself is a blaze of colour and a cacophony of noise, with every possible variety of band marching with or riding on the floats. A great day out and enormous fun.

The tulip became a symbol of Lincolnshire – when we set up BBC Radio Lincolnshire in 1980 the choice for a logo was between a tulip and a potato, and the tulip was selected. Unfortunately, tulip production in the area is now much reduced, since mechanising the crop on the Fenland soils has proved to be more difficult than on Dutch sands, with the result that tulips are now mostly grown over there, while we have concentrated on the more easily handled daffodil, which can be lifted with what is basically potato harvesting equipment. Bulbs and flowers continue to be big business: South Holland alone produces about a quarter of all the daffodils grown anywhere in the world, and the export market for flowers and bulbs is a valuable contribution to the local economy.

It is still worth a drive round the bulb fields in the spring, even though the range of colours is now more limited to a variety of shades of yellow and white, but the fields are not the only place to see them. In many villages and on the roadsides, daffodils have been planted, or just grown from discarded bulbs, and fine shows are available just by driving along. A 21st century child still has the chance to be enchanted by the flowers of the South Lincolnshire Fens.

Men of the Fens
Who was Hereward, and why was he a Wake?

Hereward is the Fens' Robin Hood; not because he took from the rich and gave to the poor, although he may have done, but because so many stories have become attached to him it would have needed several lifetimes to do it all.

The bare bones are that he was probably a South Lincolnshire landholder in the Fens and the surrounding area who lost his lands to the Normans after the Conquest, rebelled against the new rulers, but eventually lost the fight and faded out of history. Beyond that lies legend, romance and an awful lot of local and national axe-grinding!

If you believed it all, Hereward would have been born in Bourne, the son of the Earl of Mercia and his wife Godiva, of naked riding fame. Having already fallen out with the English king Edward the Confessor, he fled to Ireland; to Scotland, where he killed a bear; to Cornwall, where he slew a giant to save a maiden; and to Flanders, where he served as a mercenary and married a local girl Torfrida.

He returned to Bourne after the Conquest to find the Normans in possession of his castle and lands, having already killed Hereward's brother. Taking offence at this, Hereward killed one, several or all of the Normans and fled into the Fens, where he either joined a Danish army on the Isle of Ely, or recruited a force of his own, including a number of monks and other clerics. One or other of these groups then sacked Peterborough Abbey *'to save the treasures from falling in to Norman hands'* then retired to Ely to stage what is generally regarded as the last significant English opposition to the Normans.

The Isle was duly besieged by William's forces, who were said to have constructed a long causeway to allow access across the marshes, and there is some archaeological evidence for such a siege. Early attempts failed, possibly because the causeway was not strong enough to support mounted cavalry, and an attempt by Ivo Tailleboise, the Earl of Spalding, to gain access by witchcraft was also foiled. Eventually, however, a traitor on the English side, or a monk fed up with being marooned by the siege, let the Normans in, and Hereward took to the Fens again. For old times sake, he sacked Peterborough Abbey again then took to a life of raiding other towns and centres in and around the Fens. Oddly enough, according to one story, when he and his men got lost while attacking Stamford, they were helped by St. Peter, the patron saint of Peterborough Abbey, in gratitude for not killing the Abbot, and giving back part of what they took!

Most legends suggest that Hereward was eventually pardoned by William, with some claiming that he lived quietly in Lincolnshire, with his lands there restored to him, or that he went overseas again and died there. The more colourful story is that, despite the pardon, Hereward was attacked by sixteen Normans and, although he killed all of them, he was then stabbed in the back by another four who arrived during the fight.

In his life, and the years immediately afterwards, Hereward was usually described as 'the Outlaw' or 'the Exile', but eventually became Hereward 'the Wake'. According to the stories, this was because he was always alert and watching for danger,

but it is much more likely to have been added by the Wake family who became important landowners in the Bourne area, to add some historic gloss to their achievements.

According to Charles Kingsley, Hereward was the *'bravest, the noblest and most fearless leader that this realm has ever known'*, adding that with four such men *'the Norman power could have been overthrown'*. That seems unlikely, but the story of one man opposing authority was always likely to appeal to the anarchistic tendencies of Fenlanders – as well as small boys brought up close to Bourne!

King John's Lost Treasure

For centuries, anyone going between King's Lynn in Norfolk and Sutton Bridge in Lincolnshire would have been faced by the Holbeach and Gedney Marshes. Travellers between the two counties had either to make a long detour through Wisbech in Cambridgeshire or risk the dangerous passage across the tidal creeks, quick sands and bogs surrounding the outfalls of the Nene and the Great Ouse.

According to legend, one victim of the difficult crossing was King John. In 1216 he took the long route, but sent his baggage train across the marshes. There it was caught by the incoming tide and all the accumulated treasure of the crown, along with the wagons, his household goods and two or three thousand men were lost.

How it happened depends on which version of the story you read! There was a recognised route to be followed, but parts of it were always liable to be washed away by floods or the tides, so a good local guide was always needed to offer the most up-to-date advice. Perhaps they chose an unreliable guide, or maybe the retinue, aware of the king's temper, and the fact that he was known to be in a hurry, meant they didn't wait for guides, and just headed out on their own. Some versions of the story have it that the entourage had arrived in Lynn from Lincolnshire a few days earlier, so perhaps they made the fatal mistake of thinking that the route back would be the same as the one they took coming over.

Many treasure hunters have tried to find the lost jewels, but without success. They may still be there, buried thirty feet down in silt, or they could have been found quite quickly by locals who preferred not to advertise the fact. We will probably never know, unless one of the ever-hopeful metal detectorists who still comb the area come up with a find that would make them extremely rich.

How Lincolnshire went to Australia

A glance at a map of the South Australia coast will reveal a Kirton Point, Sleaford and Tumby Bays, a Boston Island and a Cape Willougby, all clustered around Port Lincoln. How did that group of Lincolnshire names turn up on the other side of the world? The answer lies in a remarkable group of explor-

ers and navigators from around the edges of the Lincolnshire Fens, who took to the seas in the late 18th and early 19th centuries.

The best known is Sir Joseph Banks, born at Revesby, who accompanied James Cook on his voyage round the world, described much of the flora and fauna of Australia and helped found the then-colony of New South Wales. Banks returned to Britain, and played a major part on the schemes to drain the East and West Fens.

George Bass, born near Sleaford but brought up in Boston, was a ship's surgeon who, when his ship was sent to Australia, bought his own small boat to explore the coast of New South Wales. Bass was the first to realise that there was a sea passage between the island of Tasmania and the rest of the continent. That strait is now known as Bass Strait in his honour. With another Lincolnshire-born companion, Lieutenant Matthew Flinders, he sailed through the passage in the sloop *Francis,* and they went on to circumnavigate the island. Bass is believed to have died in South America, having sailed there across the Pacific from Botany Bay.

Flinders, who came from the Fenland market town of Donington, where he is commemorated with a statue, had already visited Australia during a voyage with the ill-fated Captain Bligh, fortunately not on the *Bounty!* After the journeys with Bass he continued his explorations, leading an expedition, supported by Banks, which planned to circumnavigate Australia. The ship proved unfit for the purpose, and although he did map much of the south coast of the continent, and was probably responsible for most of the place names mentioned earlier, he was only able to survey part of the east coast before the condition of the ship forced him to give up the mapping, although he completed the circuit despite the leaks.

That was just the start of his problems. He set sail for England as a passenger on board *HMS Porpoise,* but she was wrecked on the Great Barrier Reef. Flinders took charge of one of the ship's boats and sailed it back to Sydney, from where a rescue expedition was sent for the rest of the *Porpoise*'s crew and passengers.

Flinders set out again, this time in command of *HMS Cumberland,* but more leaks forced him into the French island of Mauritius for repairs. Unfortunately, war had broken out between Britain and France, and the island's governor interned him as a possible spy. Some months later, the Royal Navy blockaded Mauritius, but it was a further year before Flinders was released. He returned home, to be reunited with his wife, who he had

LIEUTENANT FLINDERS

married nine years earlier shortly before leaving for Australia. He had tried to smuggle her on board with him, but the plot was discovered, and she had to be left behind.

Sadly, he died just a few years later, at the age of 40, but not before publishing his book *A Voyage to Terra Australis.* Flinders is often credited with being the inventor of the name Australia. The term had been used before to refer to the whole South Pacific area, but Flinders was almost certainly the first to apply it to the new land-mass. His importance to Australia is reflected in the fact that over 100 features there are now named after him.

A final link with the southern continent is that Flinders was the uncle of the Spilsby-born explorer Sir John Franklin, who served for some years as Governor of South Australia before setting off on his unsuccessful attempts to find the North-West Passage from the Atlantic to the Pacific Oceans.

HOLBEACH: HISTORIANS AND HEROES

Holbeach can claim a number of notable residents. In 1872 it was the birth-place and family home of Sir Norman Angell – born Norman Angell Lane. A precocious child, he worked for newspapers in Geneva, Paris and Ipswich before being fired for a critical article about Salvation Army General William Booth. A spell doing hard labour in California led to more newspaper work in San Fransisco, then Paris again before being appointed editor of the London *Daily Mail.* Here he continued his writing on politics and economics, for which he was awarded the Nobel Peace Prize in 1933. Ironically, his best known work *The Great Illusion,* written in 1909, set out to prove that war between the nations of Europe would be futile. The nations themselves proved his point by going to war twice over the next half century.

Another well-known Holbeachian was the antiquarian William Stukeley, born in 1687, who investigated the great prehistoric circles of Stonehenge and Avebury; as well as practising medicine in Boston and London, helping establish the Spalding Gentlemen's Society and, according to one story, becoming the first man to observe a crop circle, well before any stories of little green men from Mars.

The town also boasts the athlete Geoff Capes, twice awarded the title of the World's Strongest Man and seven times champion at the Scottish Highland Games to add to his tally of British, European, Commonwealth and Olympic titles.

To rugby, aviation and schoolboy story enthusiasts, however, there can only be one man to represent Holbeach. He is Cyril Lowe MC DFC, who is believed to be the real-life inspiration of the fictional flying ace, James 'Biggles' Bigglesworth. Born in Holbeach in 1891, Lowe was a player in the England rugby team that took the Five Nations Championships with Grand Slams in 1913 and 14. Joining the Royal Flying Corps at the outbreak of WWI, he was credited with nine 'kills', including one, for which he was awarded the MC, achieved while his plane was on fire. His aircraft was shot down in 1917, and he was injured in the crash, but he returned to international rugby the following year, and was capped 25 times for his country. His career total of tries for England (18) was a record that held for 66 years before being broken as recently as 1989 in a time when many more internationals are played every year.

This title is one in a new series by **Cottage Publications**.
For more information and to see our other titles, please visit our website
www.cottage-publications.com
or alternatively you can contact us as follows:–

Telephone: +44 (0)28 9188 8033
Fax: +44 (0)28 9188 8063

Cottage Publications
is an imprint of
Laurel Cottage Ltd.,
15 Ballyhay Road,
Donaghadee, Co. Down,
N. Ireland, BT21 0NG